HELLO!
UK
GRAPHICS

Graphic Design in the UK since the 1980s

ハロー！UKグラフィックス　1980年以降のグラフィックデザイン

有名なグラフィック作品を振り返ればすぐにわかることだけれど、UKのグラフィックデザインシーンは、音楽産業と密接な関わりがある。優れたグラフィックデザインの多くは、音楽を包むヴィジュアルとして生まれてきた。しかし、レコード・CD文化が衰退してきた現在、UKのグラフィックデザインシーンはどうなっているのだろうか。そんな疑問からこのプロジェクトはスタートした。

冬のロンドンは、噂通りの曇天で僕たちを迎えてくれた。ハイセンスなショップやギャラリー、クラブなどが集まるイーストロンドンのショーディッチとハックニーエリア。古い石畳と歴史ある建物にモダンなセンスがのっかったような街並と、カジュアルだけどエッジなファッションに身を包んだ人たち。10年ほど前までは家賃の安い荒れた下町だったが、その独特の雰囲気と安い家賃に惹かれて、若いクリエイターが集まり、街を再構築していったという。取材するデザイナーたちのスタジオもこのエリアに集中していた。取材のかたわら面白そうな本屋を覗き、見知らぬクラブに入り、彼らのクリエイター仲間とパブへ行く。そんなふうに僕たちはイーストロンドンで起こっている今一番新しいことと、その裏にどこまでも広がるデザインシーンのバックグラウンドに触れようとしていた。

過去30年のUKグラフィックデザインの歴史を知ると同時に、現在活躍するUKグラフィックデザイナーが、どんなメディアに目を向け、どんなクリエイションを作り出しているのか、じっくりと味わってほしい。始まりの疑問の答えとなる、UKグラフィックデザイナーたちの生きた言葉と数々の作品。そこからは、今世界中で最も刺激的なデザインシーンの息づかいを、きっと感じとれるはずだから。

When you look closely at the UK graphic design scene historically, it becomes clear that there has been always been a unique hybrid space of musicians and graphic designers interacting and collaborating together to produce amazing graphic design. Many notable works by leading UK graphic designers were famously born in this space and great work continues to be produced here. With the current decline in record/CD culture, what is happening to the UK graphic design scene? It was a question as such which inspired this project to begin.

A cloudy grey winter skyline welcomed the editorial team to London in 2010. Basing ourselves in the Shoreditch and Hackney areas of east London, a pocket of the city that until 10 years ago used to be a slightly rough around the edges area, which in recent years has had a new creative renaissance, where contemporary art galleries sit with clubs, unique restaurants with specialist shops and a new hub of London's creative community has developed (many of the studios in this book are also based in this part of London). Where, as with many other areas of the city, the streetscape blends historic stone paved streets and historical architecture with a modern sense of character and a young crowd wearing casual edgy fashion.

This book aims to capture the character and work of some of the design studios and creatives who have made their names in British graphic design in the last 30 years and tap into the work that is being produced here now across media. Whilst this book taps into notable works by many of the UK's well known graphic design names, it is not a comprehensive historical survey of British graphic design but an exciting snap shot of the UK graphic design scene. It also looks at how the heartbeat, character and spirit of London feed the design scene and creatives who live and work in it.

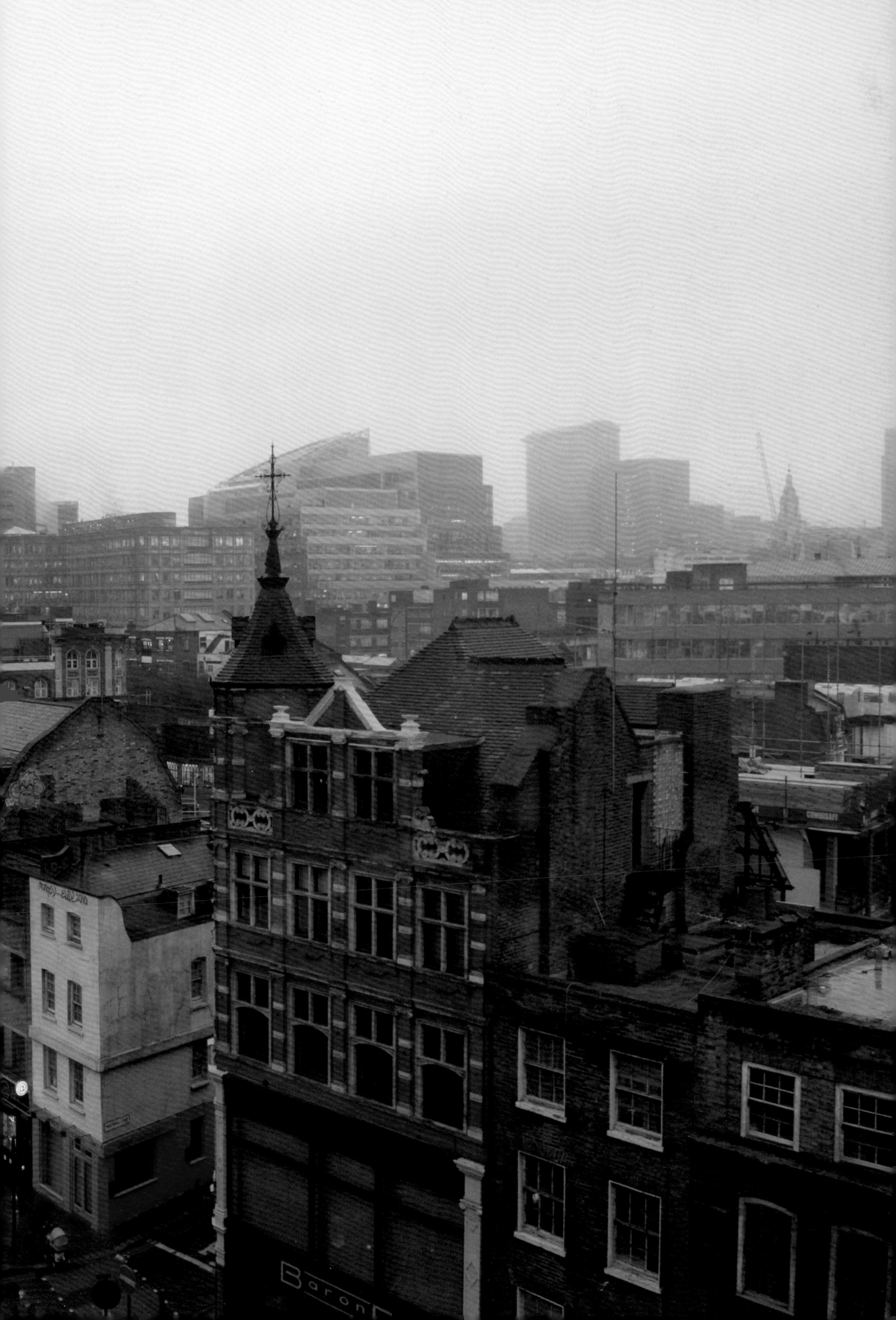
Baron

ÅBÄKE

アバケ

Åbäkeの作品には、コンセプチュアルという形容詞がしっくり馴染む。ワークショップを開催したりインスタレーション作品を展示したりと、その活動はデザイナーという範疇に収まらない。僕たちは彼らに会うために、イーストロンドン ハックニー地区へ。引っ越したばかりのスタジオは、少し散らかっていたけれど、随所から彼らのセンスが感じられる。窓からはロンドンの街が一望できた。

The adjective, conceptual, fits in nicely with Åbäke's work. Their activity exceeds the work of a designer, presenting installation work and opening workshops. We venture to Hackney, east London to meet with Åbäke. Their newly moved-in studio is a little untidy, but we're able to see glimpses of their taste amongst everything. We saw great views of London from their window.

ロイヤル・カレッジ・オブ・アートを卒業した Patrick Lacey、Benjamin Reichen、Kajsa Ståhl、Maki Suzuki の4人により2000年に設立。ミュージシャン、大学、建築家、美術館、映画制作会社、芸術財団、雑誌といった幅広いクライアントを持つ。また、この4人に、Gildas Loaëc と Masaya Kuroki を加えた6人でKitsunéを結成している。

Founded in 2000 by 4 graduates of Royal College of Art, Patrick Lacey, Benjamin Reichen, Kajsa Ståhl and Maki Suzuki. Their wide ranging clients include, musicians, architects, art museums, film production companies, arts organizations, and magazines. With Gildas Loaëc and Masaya Kuroki, the six formed Kitsuné.

(Left) An Åbäke, Made During a Residency at Tokyo Wondersite /
(Right Top) Åbäke's New Studio at 73b Regent's studio's, 8 Andrews Road, London E8 /
(Right Bottom) Our Archive in Storage (Thank you Martino) / All Photo's January 2010

"Åbäke"とは「何かと何かの間にあるもの」を意味するスウェーデン語。「グラフィックデザイナーは、作品と見る人との間の存在だから」と彼らはスタジオ名の由来を語る。メディアには顔を出さない4人組のデザイン集団。ポートレイト撮影の際には、近くにいる誰かに出演してもらうため、写る人はさまざま。時には家族写真風、時には昔の肖像画のように加工することもある。スウェーデン、フランス、イギリスと異なるバックグラウンドを持つ4人はロイヤル・カレッジ・オブ・アートで出会い、2000年の卒業と同時にスタジオを開設。『Kitsuné』レーベルの立ち上げからすべてのスリーブデザインを手掛け、広く名を知られることに。情報過多な現代社会へのアンチテーゼを込め、アルファベット1文字を使ったデザインでページを構成し世界各国の雑誌に掲載。それらの誌面を並べると文章が現れるという「スロー・アルファベット」プロジェクトなど、メッセージ性の強い作品で高い評価を受けている。

Åbäke is Swedish for, "Something in the way". "A graphic designer is a presence between the work and the viewer," explains Åbäke, as they talks about the origin of the name. They are a faceless design unit consisting of four members. For portrait photos, they ask people around them to appear, and so it's a mix. Sometimes it's shot as a family photo sometimes modified to be an old portrait. From different backgrounds, Sweden, France, and England, the four met at Royal College of Art in 2000 and established their studio soon after graduating. They became renowned designing all the record sleeves for the 'Kitsuné' record label since its inception. As an antithesis to the modern age of information overload, they have graced the pages of magazines around the globe with their one alphabet designed pages. The 'Slow Alphabet' project creates a sentence when the pages are placed alongside one another, and these impressive statements are receiving high praise.

For the font: considering in this publication and exhibition we are showing things which are appropriate in scale and material then Bell Centennial is a beautiful example of this in a typeface.
Our Slow Alphabet (see the letter Å in "The Sound Graphics" from PARCO Publishing) aims to be font one day, and though has some formal consistencies reflects our change in opinion and taste and knowledge.

Anne Tallentire ✳ THIS, AND OTHER THINGS 1999 – 2010

Irish Museum of Modern Art

1

Åbäke
www.myspace.com/
abakespace
www.kitsune.fr
www.dentdeleone.co.nz
www.sexymachinery.com

Patrick Lacey

Benjamin Reichen

Kajsa Ståhl

Maki Suzuki

a.b.a.k.e@free.fr
abakesemail@gmail.com

4

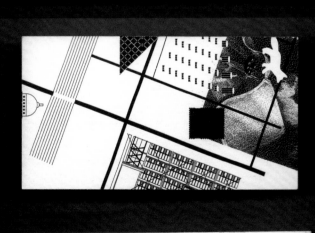

2

JohnnY Guitar ❑
Andrei Rublev ❑
Minna Tannenbaum ❑
Annie Hall ❑
Veronika Voss ❑
BarrY LYndon ❑

3

5

9

6

KITSUNÉ
åbäke

52 rue de Richelieu
75001 PARIS
T: +44 (0) 207 2492380
abake@kitsune.fr
www.kitsune.fr

7

The Film Shop
33, Broadway Market
London E8 4PH

Open, 12_10 daily
020 7923 1230

8

10

(Writer) (Artist)
Amy Prior   Sarah Doyle

I CAN'T BELIEVE HOW GREAT I FEEL

Johanna Billing's

works #3

A Great Day in Stockholm (1998)
The making of a group portrait. Disc-jockeys on the
steps of Medborgarhuset (Citizen's House), Stockholm.
....p 08

Straight from the Hip (1998) Slide projection
and magazine featuring interviews ....p 10

Graduate Show (1999) Dance video performed
by graduate students at Konstfack, University College
of Arts, Crafts and Design.......................................p 12

01

IS A WORK OF FICTION

The characterisations and incidents presented
here are products of the writer's imagination.
This story and the drawings are, however,
partly inspired by extensive, conflicting and
semi — or entirely fictional but supposedly
'true-life' celebrity reportage about the private
lives of Hollywood actors appearing in celebrity
magazines and on the Internet during 2005 and
2006 — and also (interchangeably) by their
fictional character counterparts and related
scenes from recently released Hollywood films.

: Double agents

ISBN 1-901832-21-X

Milch

9 781901 832211 >

ISBN 1-901832-21-X

BCMH
BRAVO CHARLIE MIKE HOTEL

ブラヴォー・チャーリー・マイク・ホテル

シンプルなデザインの中に潜むポップなアイデア。BCMHのデザインは、見れば見るほど、隠された物語の存在を感じさせるような奥深さに満ちている。ショーディッチ・ハイストリート駅から歩いて15分ほどの郊外にあるスタジオは、2人で使うには十分な広さ。色分けされた書籍が本棚に並び、壁際にはアート作品が置かれている。彼らの柔らかい話し方からは、デザインに対する真摯な姿勢が感じられた。

Pop-feeling ideas hidden underneath the simple design. The more you look, you get a sense of hidden stories that exist in the design of BCMH. Their studio is 15 minutes walk from Shoreditch High Street, and more than spacious enough for the two. Their books sit on shelves, colour coordinated, and art works adorn the wall. We were able to observe their sincere attitude towards design.

2004年、ロイヤル・カレッジ・オブ・アート在学中に出会ったBen ChatfieldとMark Hopkinsにより設立。まだ若いスタジオながら、ポスター、書籍、ブランドアイデンティティ、ステーショナリー、エキシビション、ウェブサイトと、その仕事は多岐に渡る。Royal College of Art、Tate Britain、Channel 4などのクライアントを持つ。

Founded in 2004, Ben Chatfield and Mark Hopkins met whilst both studying at Royal College of Art. Although the studio is young, they work in various medias, from posters, publishing, brand identities, stationary, exhibitions and websites. Their clients include Royal College of Art, Tate Britain and Channel 4.

(Left) Ben Chatfield / (Right) Mark Hopkins

Bravo Charlie Mike Hotel（BCMH）の2人によると、母校から依頼された仕事が彼らのキャリアの転機となった。「2003年秋に、ロイヤル・カレッジ・オブ・アート（RCA）を卒業してから、それぞれ別の会社で数ヵ月働いていたんだ。RCAのファウンデーションに、本のデザインをやりたいか？　と言われたのはちょうどその頃だったよ」（Ben）。RCAは毎年冬に『RCA Secret』というイベントを開催している。第一線で活躍するアーティストから若手作家まで、1000人以上の作家がポストカードサイズの作品を提供し、学内で展示販売する。その売上金が学校の基金に回されるのだが、展示販売の際、作家の名前が伏せられるから〝secret〟。BCMHは、スタジオ設立直前の2003年から、このイベントのアートディレクションを手掛けている。「最初から、僕らはすべてのことについて感覚を共有しようとしてきた。例えば仕事場のピンの色でさえもね（笑）。明確に決めたわけじゃないけど、それが僕らのスタジオのフィロソフィーかな」（Mark）。

According to the two members of Bravo Charlie Mike Hotel (BCMH), their turning point came when their old college commissioned them. "Since we graduated from Royal College of Art, we had both been working for different companies for a few months and then in the Autumn of 2003, we were asked by their foundation to design a book."(Ben). Every winter RCA host an event called 'RCA Secret'. They invite over a 1000 artists, established or up and coming, to produce a post card size work which they exhibit and sell at the college. It's "Secret" because the identity of the artist for each work remains anonymous until the after sale, the funds of which go to the college foundation. BCMH have designed this event ever since 2003, just before they set up their studio. " Since we started, we have tried to share our sensibilities. For example, even the color of the pins at our workspace (laughs). We haven't clearly defined it but this is probably the philosophy of our studio"(Mark).

1-4. RCA Secret / Postcard / Royal College of Art / 2006-9

1 / 2 / 3 / 4

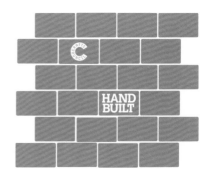

1. Sadlers Wells / Programmes / Sadler's Well Theatre
2. CC Hand Built / Identity /
Crafts Council Touring Exhibition
3. VW+BS / Brochure Design / VW+BC Architects
4. Bravo Charlie Mike Hotel /
Christmas Greeting Poster from the Studio
5. Bright One / Typographic Identity /
Bright One PR Agency
6. Yes/No / Studio Postcard

THE FIVE
BOXING
WIZARDS
JUMP
QUICKLY

ABCDEFGHIJKLMNOPQ
RSTUVWXYZabcdefghij
klmnopqrstuvwxyz012
3456789 / **ABCDEFGHIJ
KLMNOPQRSTUVWXY
Zabcdefghijklmnopqr
stuvwxyz0123456789**
/ ABCDEFGHIJKLMNO
PQRSTUVWXYZabcd
efghijklmnopqrstu
vwxyz0123456789 /
✱●★◐◑━〜━〜╱╱╱╱
THE FIVE BOXING WIZ-
ARDS JUMP QUICKLY

5

6

7 / 8

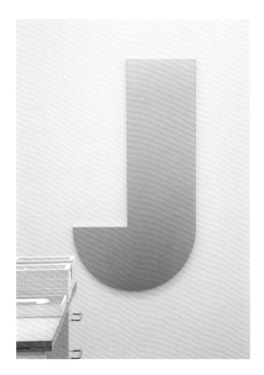

7, 8. Turner Prize: A Retrospective / Exhibition Design /
Turner Prize Retrospective Exhibition at Tate Britain
9, 10. Jerwood / Identity, Exhibition and Print Materials /
Jerwood Applied Arts Prize for Jewellery

9 / 10

BIBLIOTHÈQUE

ビブリオテーク

革新的で美しく、押し付けがましくない。Dieter Ramsの「良いデザインの10原則」を地でいくような、洗練された作品を見せてくれる Bibliothèque。デザインの基本原則を踏まえながら、モダンな感覚を通してアウトプットされるヴィジュアルは、3人のアイデアだけでなく、スタッフ全員によるディスカッションから生まれる。そんな自由でフランクな雰囲気は、インタビュー中も変わることはなかった。

Innovative and beautiful, but not imposed. Bibliothèque show us refined pieces of work, as if following Dieter Rams' 'Ten principle of design'. Their visual output, filtered through modern sensibilities and steeped in fundamental principles of design, are born out from discussion with the whole team and not just ideas from the three. That kind of free and frank atmosphere was the same during our interview.

2004年、元Farrow DesignのJonathan Jeffreyと、元NorthのMason WellsとTim Beardの3人により設立。そのモダンなデザインセンスは高い評価を得ており、Adidas、Barbican、Design Council、V&Aなど、幅広いクライアントを持つ。また、1972年のミュンヘンオリンピックを題材にしたエキシビション『72』では、企画、キュレーションを手掛けた。

Formed by a trio of designers - Jonathan Jeffrey who worked for Farrow Design, Mason Wells and Tim Beard who worked for North. Widely recognized for a reverence for modernist design principles, their varied client list includes, Adidas, Barbican, Design Council and V&A. They also self-initiated and curated an exhibition of the 1972 Olympic work of Otl Aicher.

(Left) Tim Beard / (Center) Jonathan Jeffrey / (Right) Mason Wells

1

2

1, 2, 3. Le Corbusier Exhibition /
Exhibition Design and Marketing Materials /
Barbican / 2009
4, 5. Cold War Modern Exhibition /
Exhibition Design and Marketing Materials /
Victoria and Albert Museum / 2008-2009

4/5

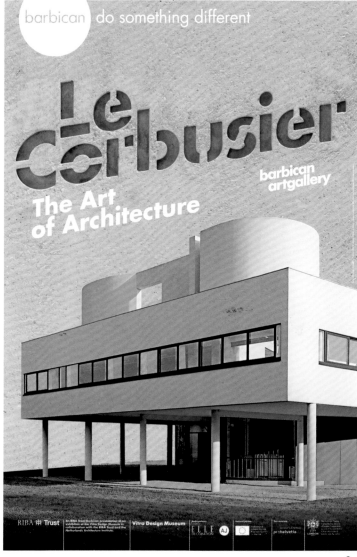

3

6, 7. 72: Otl Aicher and the Munich Plumpiad /
Exhibition Design and Marketing Materials / 2007
8, 9, 10. Super Contemporary / Exhibition Design /
Design Museum / 2009

6/7

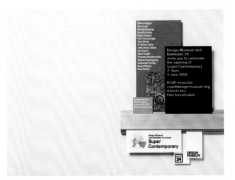

10

8/9

1

2/3

1. Adidas Olympic Archive Installation /
Exhibition Design and Marketing Materials /
Adidas in Collaboration with JJmarshall Associates / 2004
2, 3. Adicolor Installation / Exhibition Design /
Adidas in Collaboration with JJmarshall Associates / 2006
4, 5. Adicolor Book / Book /
Adidas in Collaboration with JJmarshall Associates / 2006
6. Shell / Identity / Electric Storm / 2004
7, 8. Engage / Identity System / 2008

4/5

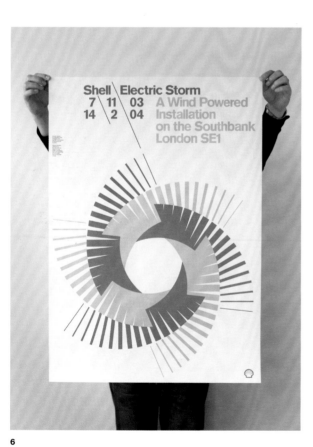

6

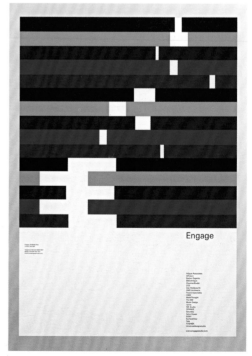

7/8

9. Dali Exhibition / Identity /
Tate Modern / 2007
10. London Sinfonietta / Identity System / 2008

9

10

11

12

11. Intersections Conference /
Identity / Design Council / 2007
12. Annual Review 07-08 / Design Council / 2008
13, 14. Moving Brands /
Guidelines and Identity / 2005

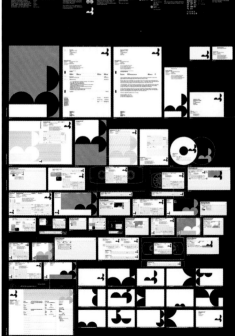

13 / 14

1

1. Covent Garden / Identity / 2008
2. Flower Cellar / Identity and Marketing Literature /
Covent Garden / 2008
3, 4. Less and More – The Design Ethos of Dieter
Rams / Exhibition Design and Marketing Materials /
Design Museum / 2009

2

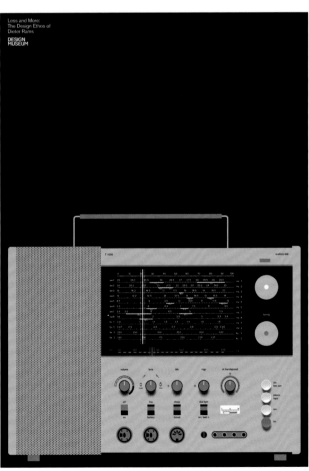

3

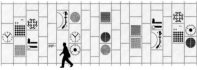

4

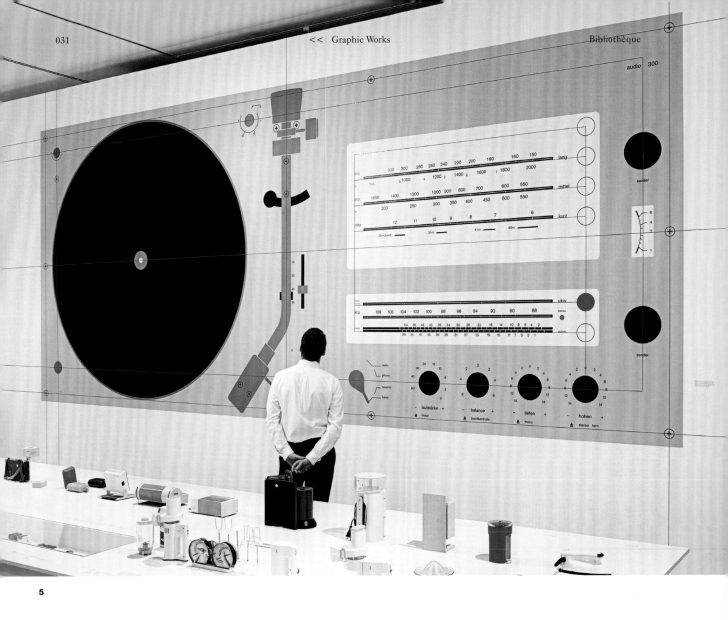

5

6   **7**   **8**

5-8. Less and More – The Design Ethos of Dieter Rams /
Exhibition Design and Marketing Materials /
Design Museum / 2009

仕事としてのデザインと、仕事を引き寄せるデザイン。

——2004年に、3人がBibliothèqueを立ち上げた理由は何でしょう?

Mason(以下、M):基本に立ち返ってリスタートしたかった、ということかな。僕たちは別々のデザインスタジオに勤めていたけれど、それを辞めて、すべて自分たちでやろうと思い立った。自分たちの好きなことをやる、そして、それをどうやって追求し、実現させていくか。それが僕たちの最初の目標であり願いだったと思う。今まで、それをすごく楽しんでやってこられた。

Tim(以下、T):Masonが言ったように、僕たちは長い間、別のデザインスタジオで働いていたから、デザインのプロセスを熟知していた。基本的な技術を持っていたからこそ、自分たちでスタジオをやろうと考えたんだ。立ち上げにあたって、仕事をどう動かしていくか、またデザイン全体をどうプロデュースするか、ということを理解していることは本当に重要だった。

Bibliothèqueから見たデザインシーン

——3人は現在のロンドンのグラフィックデザインシーンをどう考えていますか?

T:デザインを取り巻く環境は、昔と今とでは大きく違っている。10年前、20年前は、大きなデザイン会社が少数あるだけだったけれど、今はインディペンデントなデザインスタジオがたくさんあり、それぞれが切磋琢磨して、ロンドンをすごくエキサイティングな都市にしているよね。

Jonathan(以下、J):言い方を変えれば、ある種の飽和状態でもある。僕たちが学校を卒業した頃は、働きたいと思えるデザイン会社がわずかしかなかったけれど、今、卒業していたら、たくさんありすぎて迷うことになったはずさ。

スタジオの規模とクリエイティヴィティ

——今後、Bibliothèqueを大きくしていきたいという思いはありますか?

J:今、このスタジオにはスタッフが5〜6人しかいないけれど、僕たちのような小規模なスタジオの方が、よりクリエイティヴな仕事ができると思っているよ。

T:大きな会社組織は恐竜の体のようなもので、動きが鈍いだろう? 僕たちの場合は、今こうやって話しているように、お互いラフに意見を出し合いながら物事を決定していくことができる。この方が自分たちのやりたい仕事に対して、より適応できるし、より特化できる。自由で面白い感性を打ち出すこともできるんだ。もし100人のスタッフがいたら、ものすごい数の意見に耳を貸さなきゃならなくなるからね(笑)。

——少数とはいえ、デザインの方向性で意見が食い違うことはないんですか?

M:僕たちは全員、デザインに対して同じアプローチを持っているし、考え方で不一致が生じることはほとんどないんだ。スタッフをたくさん抱えた大きなデザインスタジオならいざ知らず、僕たちのスタジオにはデザインに対する明確なアプローチがあり、皆が同じイデオロギーを持っている。僕たちは個人で仕事を行うことはないし、いつもひとつのチームとして、全員がすべてのプロジェクトに加わっている。

デザインに対するアプローチ

——Bibliothèqueとしてのデザインアプローチというのは、どんなものですか?

M:例えば2009年、バービカン・アートギャラリーでの『Le Corbusier』展のときは、プロジェクト全体のキーになる要素として、本物のコンクリートに「Le Corbusier」のタイポグラフィーを刻んだオブジェクトを作った。ポスターにも写真を使っているけれど、一見しただけでは、まさか本物のコンクリートを使っているようには見えない。確かにコンピューターを使えば、簡単に作れるヴィジュアルかもしれない。だけど僕たちはあえて手間をかけて、実際に手で触れるオブジェクトを作ることを選んだ。つまり、そのコンクリートのかたまりを、プロジェクト全体を貫くデザインのキーとして使っていくことにしたんだ。こんなふうに、デザインの進むべき道を最後まで導いてくれるような、プロジェクト全体に通じるキーコンセプトを設定すること。それが僕たちのデザインフィロソフィーと言えるかもしれない。

ロンドンカルチャー界へのシグナル

——2010年2月にロンドンのデザイン・ミュージアムで開催された、インダストリアルデザイン界の巨匠、『Dieter Rams』展のグラフィックデザインも印象的でしたね。

M:この仕事をする以前から、Dieter Ramsは大好きなクリエイターのひとり。今まで僕たちは、自分たちの好きな作品、興味のある分野を、できるだけ外に

向けて発信するように努めてきた。2007年にファニチャーブランド、ヴィツゥ社のショールームで開催されたドイツのデザイナー、Otl Aicherのエキシビションは、僕たちがヴィツゥ社にアプローチして実現したもの。僕らは長年、彼の作品に強い関心を持っていたし、たくさんの本やポスターをコレクションしていたからね。『72』と名付けたこのエキシビションでは、彼のデザインチームがミュンヘンオリンピックのときにデザインした、数々の作品を展示した。こういう活動を行っていくことが、ロンドンのカルチャー界に対するひとつのシグナルになってくれる。

〝リトル・クリエイト・ネットワーク〞

──美術館やギャラリーなどのアート業界、または出版業界など、面白い企画を考えている人につながっていくということでしょうか。

J:ロンドンは、〝リトル・クリエイト・ネットワーク〞と言えるような、文化的な結びつきが強い都市だよね。

M:そうそう、ロンドンにはクリエイティヴなネットワークがあって、非商業的なレベルで好きな者同士が自然と引きつけ合う環境があると思う。Dieter RamsやLe Corbusierなど、努めて僕たちは好きなものを表明してきた。そしてそれが仕事につながっている。すごく幸運なことだ。クリエイティヴという点で面白さを感じたら、たとえ報酬がなくても仕事をする。それは僕たちの一面であり、いわばアーティストとしての活動だね。

J:それが、僕たちがBibliothèqueを始めた理由。お金のためだけにクリエイトするわけじゃない。誰かに依頼された作品でも、僕たちが好きで作っている作品でも、クリエイティヴという点では同じクオリティを保っているけどね。

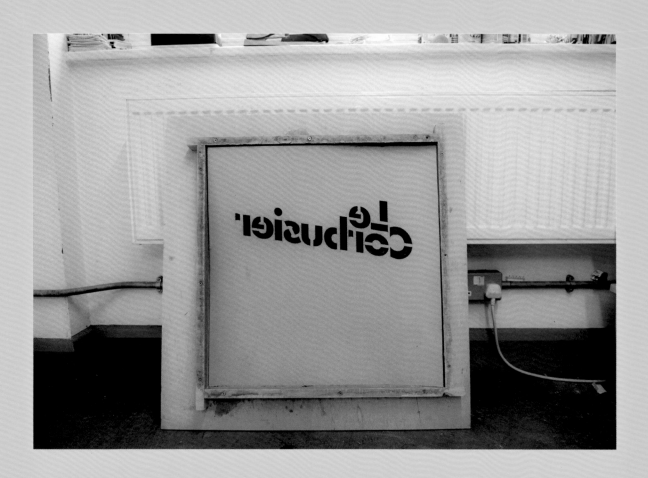

Design As Work And Design That Draws In Work.

——What was the reason the three of you set up Bibliothèque?

Mason (M): To go back to basics and start afresh. We all worked for different design studios but left our positions to do everything ourselves. To do what we wanted and work to pursue and realize those ideas. That was our primary aim and intent and up until now we have been able to enjoy doing just that.

Tim (T): As Mason said we understood the design process through our work prior in different design studios. We decided to set up our own studio precisely because we had the fundamental skills. Understanding how to move our work forward and how to produce our design as a whole was really important to the initial set up.

The Design Scene As Seen From Bibliothèque.

——How do the three of you view the current design scene in London?

T: The environment that surrounds design is vastly different now compared to the past. There were only a small number of large design offices 10, 20 years ago but now there are many small independent design studios and there is a culture of friendly competition which is making London a very exciting city.

Jonathan (J): To put it differently, it is also at a state of saturation. When we graduated from college there were only a few design offices we wanted to work for but if I had just graduated now, I would be confused as there are too many to choose from.

The Size Of The Studio And Creativity.

——Do you have ambitions of growing Bibliothèque further in the future?

J: At the moment there are only 5 or 6 members of staff at this studio but we feel a smaller scale practice like ours can produce additionally creative work.

T: A large cooperate structure is a bit like a body of a dinosaur, in their lumbered movement right? But we are able to make decisions on issues by giving our individual opinions in a relaxed way, similar to the way we are having our conversation right now. This way we're able to be more flexible and specialize in the work we want to do. This also allows us to add a more unique and free sensibility. If we had 100 members of staff we would have to listen through an awful lot of opinions (laughs).

——Even if there are only a few of you, do you disagree with the creative direction of the design?

M: As we all have a similar approach to design, we generally don't have disagreements. It may not be possible in a large design studio with a lot of staff but we all have a clear approach to design and all share the same ideology. We don't work individually on projects, but work collectively as one team and we all contribute to all projects.

Approach To Design.

——What is your approach to design at Bibliothèque?

M: For example, for the Le Corbusier exhibition at the Barbican Centre 2009, we made a concrete object with the "Le Corbusier" typography carved in as a central element to the whole project. The photograph of that was used in the poster but from first glance you wouldn't have thought it was real concrete. Of course it's easy to replicate the image using a computer but we decided to take greater care and make an object you can actually touch. So this block of concrete was central to our design of the whole project. In this way, to install a key concept which connects the whole project and lead the design the way it should be lead, could be said is our design philosophy.

Signal To The London Cultural Scene.

——The graphic design for the exhibition at the design museum in February 2010 for Dieter Rams who is a master in industrial design, was also very impressive.

M: Dieter Rams was already one of my favorite creators even before I began in this line of work. Until now we have strived to communicate the ideas of work we love and our areas of interest. The work we did in 2007 for the German designer Otl Aicher's exhibition held at the showroom of the furniture company Vitsoe was made possible because we initially approached Vitsoe directly. We had admired his work for a long time and over the years collected many of his books and posters. At the exhibition we titled '72', we chose to present many pieces of work his design team had produced during the Munich Olympics. We believe the continuation of this kind of activity becomes a signal to the cultural scene in London.

ˮLittle Creative Networkˮ.

——Would you say you begin to connect with other creative hubs such as galleries and museums in the art world or the publishing business?
J: London is a city you can call a "little creative network" as it does have a strong cultural tie.
M: Yes I agree, there is a creative network in London which has an environment where people with common interests seem to be drawn to each other on a level that isn't commercial. We have strived to present what and who we love such as Dieter Rams and Le Corbusier. And it all seems to lead to work. We're in a very fortunate position. If there were something interesting creatively, we would still work without a fee. That is one side to us, which is the work we carry out as artists.
J: And that's the reason we started Bibliothèque. We aren't creating just for the income. When it comes to the creativity we maintain the same level, whether its work we are doing because we love it or whether it's a project requested from a client.

BIG ACTIVE

ビッグ・アクティブ

ショーディッチの中心に位置するティー・ビルディング。かつては茶葉の倉庫として使われていたこのビルの7階に、Big Activeはオフィスを構えている。センスのいいサインに導かれて（あとで知ったことだが、デザインはStudio Myerscoughが手掛けている）、倉庫時代の名残を感じる大型エレベーターへ。約束の時間よりも少し早い到着だったが、創始者のGerard Saintが笑顔で僕たちを迎えてくれた。

The Tea Building is centered in the heart of Shoreditch. Big Active are located on the 6th floor of this old tea warehouse. We follow the well designed signs (we later discover these signs were designed by Studio Myerscough), to the large elevators, remnant of the warehouse days. We made an early arrival, but the founder Gerard Saint welcomed us with a smile.

1990年設立。アートディレクション、デザインのほか、イメージメイカーのマネジメントも手掛け、Sanna Annukka、Jesse Auersalo、Jody Barton、Siggi Eggertsson、David Foldvari、Matt Furie、Genevieve Gauckler、Kate Gibb、Jasper Goodall、Klaus Haapaniemi、Filipe Jardim などが所属する。2007年には、D&AD賞イエローペンシルを受賞。

Founded in 1990, the creative studio specialises in art direction and graphic design. Uniquely Big Active also represent leading commercial image makers including Sanna Annukka, Jesse Auersalo, Jody Barton, Siggi Eggertsson, David Foldvari, Matt Furie, Genevieve Gauckler, Kate Gibb, Jasper Goodall, Klaus Haapaniemi and Filipe Jardim. Winners of the D&AD Yellow Pencil Award 2007.

Gerard Saint

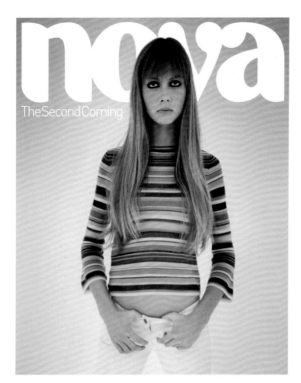

1/2

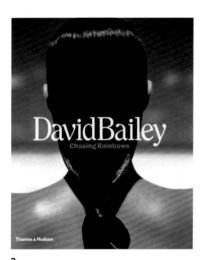

3

4/5

1, 2. Nova / Magazine / IPC Media /
AD_Gerard Saint, PH_Juergen Teller / 2000
3. David Bailey / Book / Thames & Hudson / Design
Director_Gerard Saint, PH_David Bailey / 2001
4, 5, 6. Viewpoint / Magazine / Metropolitan
Publishing (Amsterdam) / AD_Gerard Saint / 2000
4. IL_Kate Gibb
5. IL_Austin @NEW
6. PH_Sandro Sodano

TRENDS BRANDS FUTURES INTELLIGENCE IDEAS

viewpoint:

DM 120 / FF 450 / Lit 130.000 / £45

#9
FEAR
UNCERTAINTY
&DOUBT

1

2

3

4

5

6

7

8

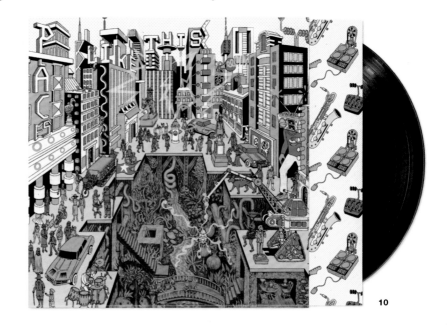

9

10

1, 2. Marina & The Diamonds / The Family Jewels /
Album / 679 Recordings / AD&Cover Art_Mat Maitland, PH_
Rankin / 2009

3. The Futureheads / Album / 679 Recordings /
London Records / AD&D_Big Active, PH_Tony Gibson / 2009

4. Kate Nash / My Best Friend Is You / Album / Fiction /
AD_Mat Maitland & Kate Nash, D_Mat Maitland, Silk
Screens_Kate Gibb / 2010

5, 6. The Freelance Hellraiser / Waiting For Clearance /
Album & Single / Brightside / AD&D_Mat Maitland,
Graphics_Jasper Goodall & Mat Maitland / 2006

7. Delays / Everything's The Rush / Album / Polydor /
D_Markus Karlsson, IL_Siggi Eggertsson / 2008

8. Goldfrapp / Black Cherry / Album / Fiction / AD_Mat
Maitland & Gerard Saint with Alison Goldfrapp, D_Mat
Maitland, PH_Polly Borland / Mute / 2003

9. Goldfrapp / Headfirst / Album / Mute / CD_Alison
Goldfrapp & Mat Maitland, D_Mat Maitland, PH_Serge
Leblon / 2010

10. Architecture In Helsinki / Places Like This / Album / V2
Co-Op, Polyvinyl / AD&IL_Will Sweeney, D_Markus Karlsson

11

14

13

12

17

16

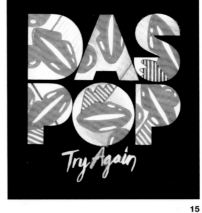

15

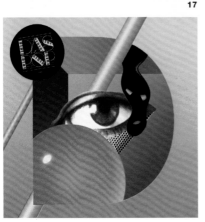

20

19

18

1

2

1, 6. Beck / The Information / CD Package with Inserted
Sticker Sheet / Interscope / AD_Mat Maitland &
Gerard Saint with Beck, D_Mat Maitland,
Sticker Images_Jody Barton, Juliette Cezzar, Estelle &
Simon, David Foldvari, Genevieve Gauckler, Michael Gillette,
Jasper Goodall, Mercedes Helnwein, Han Lee, Mat Maitland,
Ari Michelson, Parra, Melanie Pullen, Gay Ribisi,
Aleksey Shirokov, Will Sweeney, Kam Tang, Adam Tullie,
Kensei Yabuno and Vania Zouravliov / 2006
2, 3. Basement Jaxx / Scars / Album / XL /
AD&D&IL_Mat Maitland / 2009
4, 5. Basement Jaxx / Rooty_LP / Get Me Off_Single / XL /
AD_Mat Maitland & Gerard Saint, D_Mat Maitland,
IL_Rane Habermacher, Rob Kindney & Mat Maitland / 2001

3

4

5

コラボレーションが切り開く、デザインの可能性。

──Big Activeは、普通のデザインスタジオと違ってエージェンシーとしての一面も持っていますよね。

そうだね。でも組織としては、すごくシンプル。Big Activeにはデザインとエージェンシー、2つの部門がある。デザインのセクションでは、アートディレクションやデザインを行っていて、音楽や出版、ブランディングなどのプロジェクトを手掛けている。エージェンシーのセクションでは、イラストレーターをはじめとする、幅広いジャンルのクリエイターをマネジメントしている。Big Active内のデザイナーが彼らを起用することもあるし、純粋なエージェンシーとしてほかの会社との交渉役を担うこともあるんだ。

──Big Activeを始めた頃から、現在のような形態だったんでしょうか?

大学の友達と一緒にこの会社を始めた頃は、もっとトラディショナルなデザインスタジオで、ファッションブランドを中心にさまざまなジャンルの仕事を請け負っていた。1990年代になると、徐々に雑誌や書籍、そして音楽へと仕事内容がシフトしていった。それはすごく嬉しいことで、なぜなら音楽はいつも僕たちの興味の中心にあるものだったから。そして、その音楽こそが、僕たちが今まで活動してきた世界なんだ。

エージェンシーとしてのBig Active

──エージェンシーのセクションを始めたきっかけは何だったのでしょう。

1990年代の終わり頃、『Scene』というロンドンのファッション雑誌をデザインし、その後に『Nova』という音楽雑誌のリニューアルを手掛けた。そこで僕たちは数多くの才能あふれるクリエイターと一緒にヴィジュアルイメージを作ったんだ。世界でも有数の才能と仕事ができることはすごく嬉しいことだった。彼らの中には元々、個人的に付き合いのある友人もいたし、作品を目にして僕たちからコンタクトをとったクリエイターもいた。とにかく作品を見て独創的で面白いと感じたら、誰とでも一緒に仕事をしていたよ。彼らの多くがエージェンシーに所属していなかったし、彼らを理解するエージェンシーも少なかった。それなら僕たちがやるべきだ、というのが始まり。Big Activeが今の形になったのは、そんな経緯からなんだ。

唯一無二の作品かどうか

──マネジメントを始めるとき、どんな基準でクリエイターを選んでいますか?

ほかに類を見ない作品を発信しているかどうか、独創的な作家性を持っているかどうか。すごくシンプルなこと。Jasper GoodallやKate Gibbのように才能のあるクリエイターの作品を初めて見るとき、僕は、世界中のどこを探しても、こんな作品には出会えないと感じる。彼らが持つ作家性はユニークで、似た作品は二つとない。僕たちが探しているのは常にオリジネイターであって、誰かのフォロワーではないんだ。

──契約クリエイターを見ると、イラストレーターが多いように感じます。

1960年代から70年代、イラストレーションは、広告はもちろん雑誌やレコードカバーなどで今よりももっと注目を集めていたし、活躍の場がたくさんあった。1980年代になると、実験的な新しい写真のスタイルが登場してきたことで、トレンドは写真にシフトしていった。そして1990年代の終わり、再びイラストレーションが脚光を浴び始め、アートディレクターたちはブランドアイデンティティやデザインソリューションのために、イラストレーターを起用するようになった。その結果、現在はたくさんの新しいイメージメイカーとイラストレーターが再びクリエイティヴをリードする立場を担っている。僕たちも、そういう風潮を応援したいと思っていたし、実際に過去10年間、重要なクリエイティヴのツールとして、イラストレーションの後押しに力を入れてきたんだ。

デザインスタジオとしてのBig Active

──Big Activeの両輪のひとつ、デザインについてお話を聞かせてください。

Big Activeでデザインを行っているのは本当に少数。プロジェクトによってはフリーランスのデザイナーにサポートしてもらってはいるけれど、僕たちは常に小さいチームでデザインを行ってきた。現在、チームのメンバーはMat Maitland、Markus Karlsson、Valerio Oliveri、僕(Gerard Saint)の4人。それはまるでボーカル、ギター、ベース、ドラムで構成されるバンドのようなものさ。

ハイセンスなヴィジュアルを生み出す方法論

──アートディレクターのMat Maitlandは、イラストレーターとしてもBig Activeに所属していますね。

そうだね。Matはイラストレーターとしても活動していて、写真のコラージュというスタイルを追求している。Basement Jaxxなど、Big Activeが手掛けたたくさんの音楽プロジェクトで彼の作品を見ることができるよ。最近は、Kate NashというUKシンガーのキャンペーンを手掛けていて、それはKate Gibbとのコ

ラボレーションワーク。こんなふうに、プロジェクトに合わせて最適なクリエイターと組んで仕事をしていくのが僕たちのスタイル。そのプロジェクトに対して、より柔軟に、より適切に対応するために、コラボレーションするクリエイターはBig Activeに所属していない人を選ぶこともある。

――Matの仕事と言えば、Basement JaxxやGoldfrappのCDジャケットを思い出します。
音楽キャンペーンのアートディレクションというのは、アルバムカバーをデザインするだけではなくて、キャンペーンのあらゆる部分に関わっている。アナログ、デジタルを問わず、パッケージデザインや映像、交通広告などが相互に関連していて、それらを束ねたすべてをクリエイトしている。僕たちは常にアルバムが持っているスピリットをアートディレクションに反映させることを目指していて、それがキャンペーン全体を正しい方向に導いてくれるんだ。例えるなら、完璧にフィットする服を探すようなものだね。

コラボレーションワークの可能性

――アートディレクションやデザインを行うとき、Big Activeが最も大事にしていることは何ですか?
世の中にあるたくさんのデザインスタジオならどこでも、彼らなりのデザインに対する方法論を持っていると思う。もちろん、僕たちもヴィジュアルイメージを生み出すことの素晴らしさと、それが持つ力を信じているし、常にクオリティの高いヴィジュアルを追求してきた。主に僕たちが行っているのはアートディレクションであり、それぞれの仕事に最適なクリエイティヴを探すこと。即ちそれは、イメージを作るクリエイターとのコラボレーションを意味している。そしてそれは、自分たちと同じ志を持ったクリエイターの創造性が反映されるべきで、決してひとりの力だけで作り上げるものではないんだ。Big Activeがバンドだとすれば、より素晴らしい音を奏でるために、ほかのミュージシャンと協力して音作りをするようなものさ。デザイナーとイメージメイカーがお互いの良さを引き出し合い、ベストなクリエイティヴを生むこと。僕たちはコラボレーションの力を強く信じているんだ。

(Interview with Gerard Saint, creative director & founder of Big Active)

The Possibilities Of Design Opened Up Through Collaboration.

——**Big Active is different to most design studios as you also work as agents for commercial artists**

Yes. But the structure is very simple. In Big Active there are two sections - the design studio and the agency division. The creative studio works in art direction and design, mainly for music, publishing and branding projects. The agency represents illustrators and manages their commercial commissions from a wide range of outside creative professions. As designers we often collaborate with our own image makers on projects if we feel this is creatively appropriate. Otherwise with outside commissions the agency will negotiate with clients on behalf of the artist. It's all about developing and managing the artist's commercial work.

——**Did you have the same structure in place from the start of Big Active?**

When I set up Big Active with a couple of college friends we began as a more traditional design studio working mainly with fashion brands as well as undertaking graphic work in other areas. As Big Active developed in the 1990's our work began to move particularly towards magazines, music graphics and publishing. And doing more and more music design work really focused our plans as a studio, because music was something we were all really into outside of the studio. That was the world we lived in.

Big Active As An Agency.

——**What was the catalyst for staring the agency section?**

Towards the late 1990's, we were art directing a London fashion magazine called 'Scene' and working on the relaunch of a magazine called 'Nova'. Both involved commissioning a great many talented photographers, illustrators and image makers. We had the pleasure of working with some of the best photographers and image makers in the world - and amongst them we also commissioned many of our talented up and coming friends whose work we rated and admired. Many of those artists didn't have agents at the time or didn't feel there was an agency that really understood them. We soon realized that perhaps we should start that agency ourselves. That's how Big Active started representing artists as well as being designers...

Whether A Work Is Unique Or Not.

——**What are your criteria's in choosing an artist to be represented by your agency?**

The most important thing is that they have a unique visual voice - producing work that is original and thinking outside the box. It's very simple. When we first saw the work of artists such as Jasper Goodall and Kate Gibb it was clear that they were doing something different and that was incredibly exciting. Their artistry is unique and all of our artists produce very different styles of work. We are looking for originators and not followers.

——**Many artists who are with your agency seem to be illustrators.**

The 1960's and 1970's was a incredible time with lots of opportunities and commissions for illustrators - their work being used extensively for editorial, record covers and advertising. In the 1980's the trend moved much more towards photography as lots of new photographic styles were being experimented with. The late 1990's saw a reversal in this to some degree with art directors choosing once more to use illustration as a way to create a defining look for design solutions and brand identities. As a result illustration has once more taken a more leading roll with many new images makers coming through - we'd like to think that we played a part in encouraging that. And for the last ten years our agency has focused on promoting illustration as a vital creative medium.

Big Active As Design Studio.

——**Can tell us about the design side of Big Active.**

We have always worked as a small creative team - driving the art direction and design side of the studio - currently this consists of Myself (Gerard Saint), Mat Maitland, Markus Karlsson and Valerio Oliveri. That's the line up of the band - vocals, guitar, bass and drums.

Methodology Behind Creating A Sophisticated Visual Identity.

——Your art director Mat Maitland is also represented Big Active as an illustrator, is that correct?

Yes. Mat also works as an illustrator developing his style of photo-collage. You can see his work in many past Big Active projects including Basement Jaxx. Recently he has been working in collaboration with Kate Gibb on our campaign for the UK singer "Kate Nash". This is a good example of our art direction style collaborating with different artists depending on the project. Also we sometimes choose to work with artists who are not with Big Active, the idea is to be flexible and react appropriately to each individual project.

——When I think of Mat's work, I remember the CD covers for Basement Jaxx and Goldfrapp.

Art direction for a music campaign consists not only about designing the defining image of the cover art but also all of the integrated aspects of the visual campaign. It's important to consider all of the mutually connected elements, such as the visuals, package design and advertising - both in print and digital - and these create the story surrounding the total package. We always aim for our work to reflect the spirit of the albums that we design right across the campaign - finding the clothes that fit perfectly.

Possibilities In Collaboration.

——What is the most important thing for Big Active when you are involved in design or art direction?

There are many design studios that have a unique methodology in their design. For example they have a particular visual signature style and this is very much reflected in the work produced. Our work is all about art direction and finding appropriate creative solutions - of course we're interested in having a really strong visual voice - and we use collaboration as a way of achieving this. We love working with artists who share the same vision - design is all about teamwork - I like to think of Big Active as a band, and working with other creative artists is like making more ambitious music with a wider scope of different musicians. We believe in collaboration. It's about bringing out the best creative work in both designer and image maker.

(Interview with Gerard Saint, creative director & founder of Big Active)

EAT SLEEP WORK/PLAY

イート・スリープ・ワーク／プレイ

人文字でアルファベットを作ったり、オモチャをモチーフに使ったりと、Eat Sleep Work/Play(ESW/P)のデザインには、見る人の気分を明るくする〝遊び〟があふれている。4人でシェアする(ESW/Pは2人組)スタジオは、天井が高く気持ちのいい空間。インタビューの合間にジョークを交えるZamir Antonioと、優しい笑顔が印象的なAntoine Choussat。その人柄は、作品の雰囲気そのままだった。

The designs of ESW/P, whether it be human letter alphabets or using toy and mirror motifs, are full of "charm" that brighten the feeling of the viewer. The studio shared by the four (ESW/P are a duo), have high ceilings and are light and spacious. Zamir Antonio mixes in jokes during the interview and a smiley Antoine Choussat looks on. Their personalities were exactly like the mood of their works.

2006年にセント・マーチンズ、2008年にロイヤル・カレッジ・オブ・アートを卒業した2人、フランス・パリ出身のAntoine Choussatと、アメリカ生まれスイス出身のZamir Antonioにより設立。Apple、Adidas、Puma、VH1、Pepsiなどをクライアントに持つほか、母校のセント・マーチンズや、キングストン大学にて教鞭もとっている。

Founded by Antonie Choussat from Paris, France and American born Swiss bred Zamir Antonio, who both graduated Central St. Martins in 2006 and Royal College of Art in 2008. Apart from working with clients which include, Apple, Adidas, Puma, VH1 and Pepsi, they also teach at Central St. Martins and Kingston University.

(Left) Zamir Antonio / (Right) Antoine Choussat

Eat Sleep Work / PlayのZamirとAntoineは2003年にセント・マーチンズで出会った。「入学して最初の週に意気投合し、一緒に作品を作るようになったんだ」（Zamir）。大学内のプロジェクトなどでコラボレーションを続けるうちにクライアントを得るようになり、『A MAGAZINE - curated by YOHJI YAMAMOTO』にも参加。その後7年間、創作活動を続け、最近ではアップル社の広告キャンペーンを手掛けるメディア・アーツ・ラボでアートディレクターとして活躍。そのかたわら、セント・マーチンズで教鞭もとっている。学生時代から多くの仕事をこなし、若くしてすでに名を成した2人。彼らのデザインそのものの魅力はもちろんのこと、成功の秘密はフットワークのよさにもあるのではないだろうか。スタジオ名は「いつもやっていることを名前にすることにした」（Antoine）と、飄々としたもの。"WORK / PLAY"という表現も、仕事と遊びが彼らにとって不可分であることがうかがえて面白い。

Antoine and Zamir of Eat Sleep Work/Play met at Central Saint Martins in 2003. "We hit it off from the first week we started and began working together"(Zamir). Enthusiastically collaborating on college projects and live briefs, the duo gradually began acquiring their first clients while studying, and were even invited to contribute to 'A MAGAZINE curated by YOHJI YAMAMOTO'. Soon to be almost seven years later, they continue to build steadily on their practice producing admirable work, recently also working as art directors at Media Arts Lab on the global Apple account as well being associate lecturers at Central Saint Martins. They have made a name for themselves fairly young, working on many projects since their student days. Of course the secret to their success may lie in their attractive designs, but by also being immensely light-footed. "Our name comes from what we always do," says Antoine lightheartedly. As you can tell from the expression "Work/Play", it's amusing to see that work and play is an integral part of them.

1. Kokon To Zai / London Fashion Week Visual / 2007
2. Kokon To Zai / Store Cards / 2005-2009
3. Modular Weekly / Poster / 2007

1

2

3

056

1. Royal College of Art /
Design Interactions Publication / 2007
2. Wiley / My Mistakes Single Artwork / 2007
3. YCN / 72 Rivington Street Branding / 2009
4. Marjan Pejoski /
Spring-Summer 08 Lookbook / 2007
5. University of the Arts / Rebranding / 2006
6. KTZ / Spring-Summer 07 / 2006
7. Gareth Pugh / Aftershow Party Invite / 2007

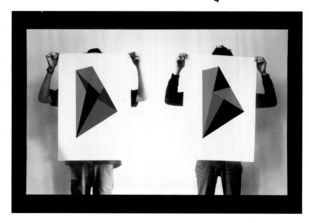

1

2

3

4

5

6

7

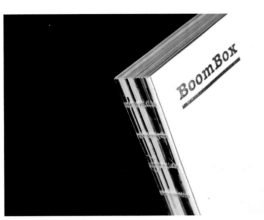

8

9

10

12

11

8. Royal College of Art /
Design Interactions Publication / 2008
9. Boombox / The book / 2007
10. Modular Records / Visual / 2007
11. The Arguing Alphabet / ESWP / 2004
12. Central Saint Martins /
Fashion Womenswear Publication / 2007

INTRO
JULIAN HOUSE

イントロ（ジュリアン・ハウス）

細い階段を登りきり少し緊張しながらドアを開けると、古いオーディオ機器やTVのオブジェと、大企業のようなレセプションが目に入る。Introは、デザインだけでなく映像専門のチームも持つ大きなスタジオだ。インタビューに応じてくれたのは、OasisやPrimal Screamなどのアートディレクションを手掛けるJulian House。僕たちが投げかける質問に対して、静かにそして丁寧に彼は答えてくれた。

A little nervous, we walk up the narrow stairs and opened the door to see the large company-like reception with old audio equipment, TV and objects. Intro are a large studio with not only graphic, but a specialized video team. Julian House, art director to projects which include Oasis and Primal Scream, accepted our interview. He answered our questions we threw at him in a friendly and kind natured manner.

1988年設立。主に、音楽プロジェクトのアートディレクションを手掛け、スリーブデザインはもちろんミュージックビデオでも数々の賞を受賞している。音楽のほかにも、コマーシャルフィルム、ファッション、アートなど、幅広い分野で活動。シニアデザイナーのJulian Houseは、Oasis、Primal Scream、Broadcastなどのアートディレクションを手掛ける。

Founded in 1988. They mainly specialize in art direction for music projects, also winning numerous awards in sleeve design and music videos. Aside from music, they work in broad range of areas such as commercial film, fashion, and art. Senior designer Julian House has art directed Oasis, Primal Scream and Broadcast among others.

Julian House

1

2

3

8. Live Earth / Animated Sting
9, 10. Primal Scream / Beautiful Future /
Album Campaign
11. Primal Scream / XTRMNTR / Album Campaign
12. Primal Scream / Evil Heat / Album Campaign

8

9

10

11

12

1 / 2

3

4

Ghost Box
The Transactional Dharma of

A TENDER SPIRIT

TECHNOLOGY IS...
NEVER SEEMED TO BE SO FAR AWAY.

Ghost Box
We are all
Pan's People
The Focus Group

Ghost Box 05

hey
let loose
your
love
The Focus Group

5 / 6

7

01 Farmer's Angle
Belbury Poly
02 Sketches and Spells
The Focus Group
03 The Willows
Belbury Poly
04 Ouroborindra
Eric Zann
05 Hey Let Loose
Your Love
The Focus Group
06 Mind How You Go
The Advisory Circle
07 The Owls Map
Belbury Poly
08 We are all
Pan's People
The Focus Group
09 The Séance at
Mons Lane
Mount Vernon Arts Lab

"Some of the most
delightful electronica to
arise in Britain since
Aphex Twin, the Black Dog
and Global Communication
in the early 1990s."

Sunday Times

"By accessing the disquiet
of Britain's other hidden
reverie, Ghost Box trace
an alter-effect of the
relationship between high
modernism and populist
thought that was endemic
to British culture
between the 1950s and
1970s. This makes it easy
to trace key influences
you can hear the BBC
Radiophonic Workshop,
Basil Kirchin, The Wicker
Man soundtrack and so on."

Frieze Magazine

"Ghost Box are weird
England in exile. Each
release gives us another
glimpse into their alter-
native Albion."

Fact Magazine

"What is returned to us
(assuming, perhaps, that
you're British and grew
up in the 1960s and
1970s) is a sense of
this country, and a
stranger, more fantasti-
cal place than you had
ever realised: Homeland
becomes unheimlich."

Frieze Magazine

The Ghost Box Periodical 01

A varied program of
musical activities for
educational and ritual
use.

Starts January 2005

Folklore and Mathematics

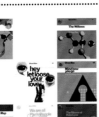

06...

Module 06
The Advisory Circle   Mind How You Go

Timely advice from
The Circle
Remember, electricity can
not be seen or heard.
Harmful, invisible forces
surround us everywhere
we go.

October 2005

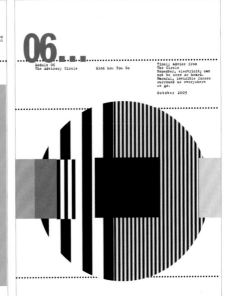

Monday, JUNE 14 1971

OAKSTON MAST BLAMED FOR BELBURY BUZZ

Dickie Mincham reports

Associations
& Networks
1958-1978

WHAT ARE
YOU SEEING
MIND HOW
YOU GO

The engineers of the
B.B.C. do not write
the programmes which
they send out. They
are the power which
sends out the broad-
cast. They are not
even the machines
which take the photo-
graphs. Yet their
minds are necessary
before the broadcast
can take place. It
is probably much the
same with the produc-
tion of ghosts.

Detective Inspector Wells

T.C. Lethbridge
Ghost and Ghoul

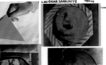

09

Module 09
Mount Vernon Arts Lab   The Séance at Mob's Lane

A séance of great artists
under the guidance of a
visionary, medium and...

Ghost Box.co.uk

8 / 9 / 10

1 / 2 / 3 / 4

5

6

1-4. Oasis / Dig Out Your Soul / Album Campaign
5. Oasis / Worldwide Tour / Programme
6. Oasis / Promotional Playing Cards
7, 8. Oasis / Falling Down / Single Art
9. Oasis / Worldwide Tour / Poster

7 / 8

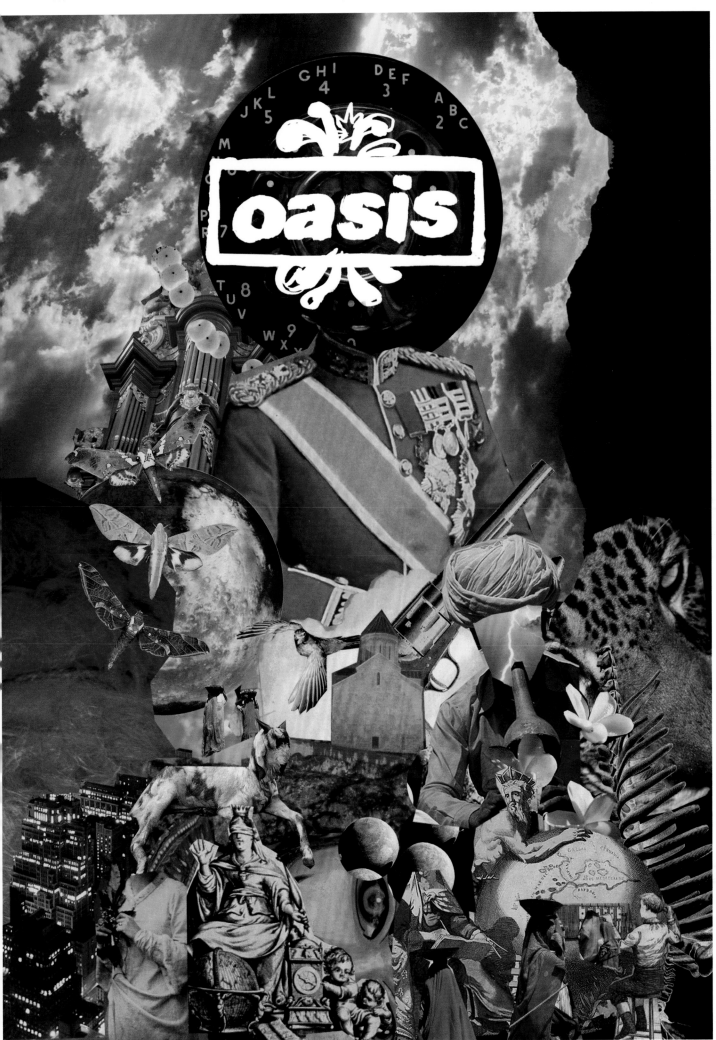

過去の文化を切り出して生まれる、新しいデザイン。

──まず、あなたがグラフィックデザイナーという仕事を選んだ経緯を教えてください。

子どもの頃から、たくさんのレコードスリーブやコミックなど、ヴィジュアルカルチャーに囲まれて育ったので、ずっとアートを勉強したいと思っていたんだ。ウェールズ大学ニューポート・カレッジに入学し、そこでヴィジュアルワークを仕事にする方法のひとつとして、グラフィックデザインの存在を知った。大学ではヴィジュアルワークに関するさまざまな手法を試し、試行錯誤の末、コラージュというファインアーティストが使っていた古い手法をグラフィックデザインに応用するようになった。その後、セント・マーチンズの修士過程で学んでいるとき、長年抱いてきたポップカルチャーへの関心を仕事に反映させるためには、音楽産業が一番適していると考えたんだ。それで、友人がやっていたBroadcastというバンドの、シングルスリーブのデザインを手掛けた。それがグラフィックデザイナーとしての初仕事だね。

Introを選んだ理由

──セント・マーチンズ修了後、Introへ入ったのですか?

多分、1996年頃だったと思うけど、学生時代の作品が大半を占める自分のポートフォリオを持ってここにやってきたんだ。Introを選んだのは、大学時代に思い描いていた仕事をやるのに、最もふさわしい場所だと思ったから。Introは音楽分野に強いデザインスタジオだったし、それ以外にもたくさんの実績があったしね。実際ここでは、スリーブデザインだけでなく、ミュージックビデオや広告、ギャラリーをベースにしたアートワークなど、たくさんの要素がクロスオーバーしたプロジェクトを手掛けている。

──入社してみて、Introという会社にどんな印象を持ちましたか?

Introのデザイナーのひとり、Mat Cookが手掛けた音楽レーベル『Blood & Fire』のスリーブデザインが印象に残っている。それは、彫刻とコラージュ、タイポグラフィーを組み合わせたもので、1960年代の雑誌『Graphics』を思い出させるようなグラフィックワークだったんだ。そしてそれは、デザインに対して持っていた自分なりの視点や考え方にフィットするものだった。

Sonic Youthのレコードスリーブ

──あなたのキャリア形成上、デザインにおいて特に強烈に影響を受けたものは何でしょう?

僕のキャリアの根底には、ポップカルチャー、それもレコードスリーブの優れたデザインが存在している。ニューポート・カレッジ時代は、表現性豊かなタイポグラフィーとコラージュワークによるSonic Youthのスリーブが大好きだったんだ。これこそが自分のやりたいスタイルだと思ったね。それらのスリーブデザインには、感情をデザインに変換するような、ビートカルチャーやポップアートの影響が見てとれた。当時の作品のほとんどがコラージュをベースにしたもので、自分をグラフィックデザイナーではなくイラストレーターと呼んだ方がふさわしいくらい、コラージュばかりやっていたよ。初めてタイポグラフィーを扱ったのは、セント・マーチンズに入ってからだった。

1960年代ポップカルチャーの影響

──あなたの一連のコラージュワークを見ると、どこか共通した雰囲気を感じます。

今までやってきた仕事はアーティストやミュージシャンとのコラボレーションが多く、基本的には彼らと話し合いながら制作しているけれど、クリエイションの底には、古い書籍やレコードなど、たくさんのポップカルチャーの集合体が存在している。特に、1960年代カルチャーからの影響が色濃く、当時のポップミュージックや、William S. Burroughsを通して見えるビートカルチャーの世界観、アンダーグラウンドシネマの世界観が多分に含まれている。1960年代のデザインを見ると、ルールはあるけれどデザインの解釈そのものがもっと幅広かったように感じられる。例えば、狂ったように抽象的なデザインや、今では考えられないようなタイポグラフィーなど、それらは僕が今やっているスタイルに近いものだね。

音楽キャンペーンの肝

──音楽キャンペーンのデザインを手掛ける際に、どんなプロセスで進めているのか教えてください。

さっき話したように、制作の最初のステップはミュージシャンとの対話。コラージュ要素となるたくさんのイメージソースを彼らに投げかけながら、創作の引き金になるようなベースをまず作る。そして、その後でヴィジュアルを整えていく。音楽キャンペーンの肝は、スリーブのフロントカバーにあると僕は思っているんだ。それはまさに創造の入り口と言えるもの。だからこそキャンペーン全体に通じるアイデンティティを体現するものであると同時に、一枚のヴィジュアルとし

ても、強さがあるものでなければならない。最初に作ったカバーデザインを元に、スリーブ中面や映像など、関連するすべてのものに派生させていく。そうすることで、キャンペーン全体のさまざまな要素を同じ文脈上に位置させることができるんだ。

——Primal Scream『Beautiful Future』のCDスリーブも、とてもインパクトがありました。

『Beautiful Future』は、イタリアのホラー映画とチープなVHS映像のイメージを元にしている。すべてのヴィジュアルに、古い映像にしばしば見られるノイズラインを施し、チープなビデオモニターを通したようなイメージに仕上げた。例えるなら、David Cronenberg監督の代表作『VIDEODROME』のような雰囲気だね。同じくPrimal Screamの『XTRMNTR』では、ベトナム戦争当時のアメリカ軍や軍事産業の思想をテーマにした。それに加えて、初期のTVゲームやCNNが放送していた番組映像、ドラッグ中毒者の幻聴や妄想のイメージもミックスしている。たくさんの異なるイメージを衝突させると、その真ん中に作品が生まれるんだ。

"手"でしか生み出せないもの

——グラフィック作品と映像作品で、制作プロセスに違いはありますか?

異なるプロセスもあるけれど、根本的な考え方は同じ。コラージュのパーツは、それぞれが物語を持っていて、それらを相互に関連づけるように編集して作り上げていく。この点はフィルムでも同様で、Primal Scream『Kill All Hippies』のフィルムは、ある部分は現代のフィルムから、ある部分は50年前のフィルムからというふうに、異なる映像を素材に、カットアウトして全体のストーリーを作り上げていったんだ。それと、プリントワークでもフィルムワークでも、コンピューターやフォトショップだけでは不可能なアナログとデジタルをミックスした手法をとっている。どちらの場合も、コンピューターから離れて制作するハンドメイドの過程を大事にしているんだ。なぜなら、自らの手で作る過程が、コンピューターでは不可能な生々しさを、作品に吹き込むと思っているからね。

New Design, Carved Out Of Past Cultures.

——**Firstly, can you tell us how you become a graphic designer?**

Growing up, I was surrounded by visual culture, a lot of record sleeves and comic books, and I was always keen to study art. I attended Wales University, Newport, and learnt of graphic design as a way of doing visual work as a career. At college I tried out a lot of different visual methods, and after some trial and error, began applying collage, a method used by past fine artists, to graphic design. After, whilst studying my masters at St. Martins, I ended up gravitating toward music industry design most suited to the pop-cultural world I was always interested in. I began by designing single cover for my friend's band called Broadcast. So that was my first work as a graphic designer.

The Reason For Choosing Intro.

——**Did you join Intro after graduating from St. Martins?**

I think it was around 1996 when I went into Intro with my portfolio, mostly college works. I chose Intro because I saw it as somewhere to fit in with the work I was approaching at that time in college. Intro was working a lot on the music side of things, and besides that, had a great track record. Here, we don't just take only record covers, but our projects crossover into music videos and advertising to gallery based art work.

——**What was your impression upon joining a studio like Intro?**

Mat Cook, who is a designer here, worked on a series of record sleeves for a record label called 'Blood and Fire' and I was very interested in his designs. It was a combination of sculpture, collage and typography and was reminiscent of some work I'd seen in the 1960's magazine 'Graphics'. And that, fitted in with the view and the way I think about design.

Sonic Youth Record Sleeves.

——**In your career, what has strongly influenced your design?**

At the basis of my career, there is pop-culture and great record sleeve design. When I was at college in Newport, I loved the collage based, very expressive typography of the Sonic Youth record sleeves. In those sleeve designs you could see the influence of beat-culture and pop art, almost like emotion translating into design. My work at that time was mostly collage based, so much so that you could say I was more an illustrator than a graphic designer. The first time I started using typography was after I started at St. Martins.

The Influence Of 1960's Pop-Culture.

——**Looking through your past collage work, you notice a kind of common thread.**

The jobs I had done tended to be collaborations with artists and musicians, so I usually work with them through discussion, but the basis of my work stems from old books and records, various forms of pop-culture. Especially the influence of 1960's culture remain strong, including pop music of the day, the beat-world of William S. Burroughs and underground cinema. If you look at the deign of the 1960's, there are rules, but it felt like the understanding of design itself was much broader. Things like, crazy abstract designs and typography unimaginable today. Those are close to the style I have today.

Importance In Music Campaigns.

——**What is your working process when you are designing a music campaign?**

As I mentioned before, the first step is to have dialogue with the musician. Then I might start throwing visual references, and build a base to act as a sort of trigger. Then I arrange the visuals. I think the main thing for a music campaign is the front record sleeve design. It's an opening into the world you create. So, the front cover has to identify and work visually with the whole music campaign and must stand up as a strong single image. Taking the first cover design as a basis you can then start developing everything else that relates to that, like the inner sleeve or video. Then you're able to bring all the other elements from the whole campaign together into the same context.

——The CD sleeve for Primal Scream's 'Beautiful Future' made a strong impact.

'Beautiful Future' was based on a look of an Italian horror movie and images from cheap VHS footage. Using the noise lines from the old footage, we finished all the visuals as if they had been filtered through cheap video monitors. Similar to David Cronenberg's 'Videodrome'. Again, Primal Scream's 'XTRMNTR' was based on the war and military industry of the American army at the time of Vietnam. In addition, there are images of old video games, CNN channel footage and hallucination of drug addicts crossed in. When all these references collide, the work is born in the middle.

Things Only Made Possible By Hand.

——Is there any difference in the process, between graphic design and video work?

They do involve different processes, but fundamentally they are similar. In collage, each part has a narrative, so you edit them together making connections between them. In this sense a film is the same. In Primal Scream's 'Kill All Hippies' I used different source material, one part was from a recent film and another from a 50 years old film, and cut them to build a story. Also in print or film work, I use a mix of analog and digital techniques, which you cannot achieve with just a computer or Photoshop. In both cases, I regard hand craft to be very important and not to just stick with the computer. Because I think that process gives work off the computer a bit of life.

IT'S NICE THAT

イッツ・ナイス・ザット

デザイナーを紹介する本書の中で、唯一、編集者の肩書きも持つIt's Nice Thatの2人。彼らのスタジオは、高感度なアパレルショップやギャラリーなどが集まるオールド・ストリートエリアに位置する。自分たちが気になるもの、面白いと思ったものをブログや書籍で紹介し続ける彼らにとって、ふさわしい場所なのかもしれない。若くして注目を浴びる彼らの将来に、期待を感じずにはいられなかった。

In this book introducing designers, only the duo of It's Nice That have the title of editor. Their studio is situated in the Old Street area where high-end boutiques and galleries gather. It maybe suits the duo who continue to publish or blog what they find interesting or intriguing. We couldn't help but expect good things for the youthful pair, who are attracting attention.

2007年、2人の編集者兼アートディレクター、Alex BecとWill Hudsonにより設立。ブログ形式で、さまざまなクリエイションを紹介するウェブサイトとしてスタートしたが、現在では雑誌『It's Nice That』や書籍『If You Could Collaborate』などを出版するほか、エキシビションなどの企画制作、広告プロジェクトのディレクションも手掛けている。

Founded in 2007 by two editor/art directors, Alex Bec and Will Hudson. They began as a website introducing various creations in blog format, but now also publish their magazine 'It's Nice That' and book 'If You Could Collaborate' and furthermore, curate and produce exhibitions as well as directing commercial projects.

(Left) Will Hudson / (Right) Alex Bec

Will HudsonとAlex Becの2人によるIt's Nice That。アート作品からビデオクリップ、イベント、プロダクトまで、有名無名を問わず〝It's Nice That（それ、いいね）〟と思ったものを同名のウェブサイトで取り上げ、ほぼ毎日更新している。最近ではグラフィックデザイン、アート業界でも名を知られるようになり、アーティスト同士のコラボレーションをテーマにした『If You Could Collaborate』というエキシビションをキュレーション。それをきっかけにアーティストのマネジメントも始めるなど、その活動は広がりを見せている。ブライトン大学在学中に知り合った2人は、『If You Could』プロジェクトを学生時代にスタートさせた。ウェブだけでなく出版や広告のデザインも手掛けるが、「デザインというものを、まだよくわかっていない。自分たちの好きなことをしているだけさ」とAlex。ひとつのウェブサイトから、さまざまなプロジェクトを展開させていくグラフィックデザイナーの新しい形。彼らの今後から目が離せない。

It's Nice That are Will Hudson and Alex Bec. Their daily updates website include art work and video clips, to events and new advertising campaigns and products, they pick up on anything they find that fits their "It's Nice That" ethos, whether those things are famous or not. Recently, they have become known in the art and graphic design industry, and curated the exhibition called 'If You Could Collaborate', which encouraged collaboration between artists. They are expanding their horizons, and starting to take on more work as an agency. The pair met at Brighton University, and started their 'If You Could' projects at that time. They work on websites to publishing and advertising, but Alex insists, "We don't fully understand design yet. We're just doing what we love". They are a new form of designers, developing various projects from one website. They're progression is attracting attention.

2

3

1. It's Nice That Issue 1 Poster / Print Liberation / 2009
2. Nice T-Shirt / Jean Jullien / 2009
3. New Math Mug / Craig Damrauer / 2009

1

1

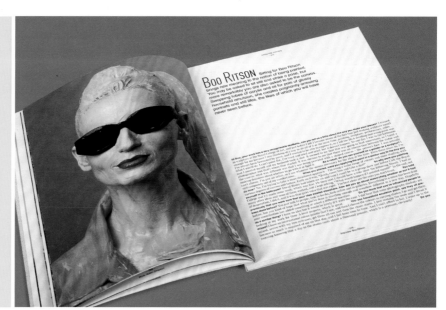

2

3

1. It's Nice That Issue 1 / Book / D_ It's Nice That in
Collaboration with Joseph Burrin / 2009
2. It's Nice That Issue 2 / Book / D_ It's Nice That in
Collaboration with Joseph Burrin / 2009
3. It's Nice That Issue 3 / Book / D_ It's Nice That / 2010

4. It's Nice That Issue 3 Poster / Parra / 2010
5. It's Nice That Issue 2 Poster / Rob Ryan / 2009
6. If You Could Collaborate / Exhibition / A Foundation
Gallery at Rochelle School / London 2010

JONATHAN BARNBROOK

ジョナサン・バーンブルック

午前10時、真っ赤なドアを開けると、そこにJonathan Barnbrookの姿はなかった。約束の時間を勘違いしていた彼が現れたのは、約30分後。丁寧な謝罪をいただいた後、急ぎ足でインタビューが始まった。書籍や雑誌で彼が見せてきたラディカルな発言の印象から、少し気難しい人柄を予想していたが、その語り口は真摯で理知的。時間は少し短かったけれど、とても豊かで濃密な時間を過ごすことができた。

At 10AM, we open the bright red door, to find Jonathan Barnbrook absent. He had mistaken our arranged time and arrived half an hour later. After receiving a very courteous apology, the interview started immediately. We had expected somebody slightly difficult due to the impression we had from the radical opinion in magazines and newspapers, but his manner of speaking was sincere and intellectual. Time flew by, but we managed to spend a productive and fruitful time.

1988年にセント・マーチンズ、1990年にロイヤル・カレッジ・オブ・アートを卒業。書籍、企業アイデンティティ、CDスリーブ、ウェブサイトなど幅広い分野で活躍。日本ではアーティストDamien Hirstとのコラボレーションワークや六本木ヒルズのロゴなどで知られている。1997年には、自らデザインしたフォントを発表するVirusFontsを設立した。

Graduated from St. Martins in 1988, and Royal College of Art in 1990. Working in a wide range of areas from publishing, corporate identities, CD sleeves and websites. Widely regarded in Japan for his collaborative work with Damien Hirst and the Roppongi Hills identity. In 1997, he set up VirusFonts, releasing his original fonts.

Jonathan Barnbrook

1. Adbusters Billboard: Designers Stay Away From
Corporations That Want You To Lie For Them /
Billboard / 2001
2. Mason (formerly Manson) / Typeface / 1992
3. Cult Of Virus / Catalogue /
Virusfonts / 1997

1

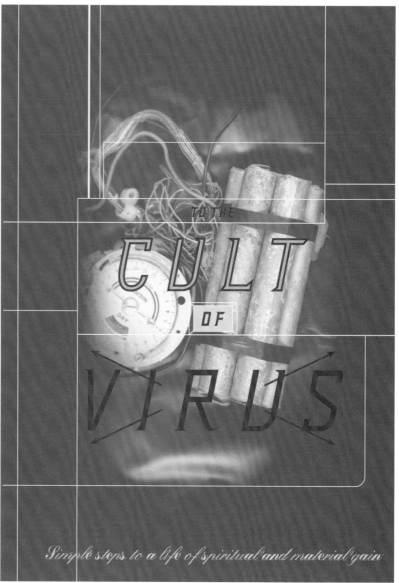

2

3

DESIGN EGO

DESIGNERS ARE FALLING OVER EACH OTHER TO KISS CORPORATE ASS

our humanity has become DISLOCATED

Do you remember the time when your car didn't have a cupholder and a regular coffee was just that? You know - regular.

"I have tried to find other designers, but I can't find anyone with his humour, irony, irreverence, and wit. Philippe always pulls new rabbits out of a hat." Ian Schrager

Design is now a fashion system.

You see it, don't you?

Image Copyright © Barnbrook Design

4. Adbusters 'Design Anarchy' Issue / Magazine
Spread / Editor_Kalle Lasn / 2001
5. KJI / Artwork / 2004
6. Shock & Awe: Tomahawk / Typeface / 2004
7. You Can't Bomb An Idea / Limited Edition
Screenprint / 2004

5

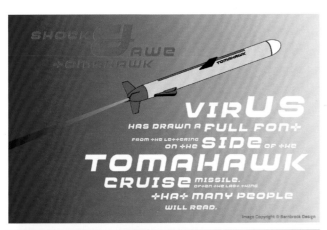

SHOCK & AWE +TOMAHAWK

VIRUS HAS DRAWN A FULL FONT FROM THE LETTERING ON THE SIDE OF THE TOMAHAWK CRUISE MISSILE. OR ON THE LAST THING THAT MANY PEOPLE WILL READ.

Image Copyright © Barnbrook Design

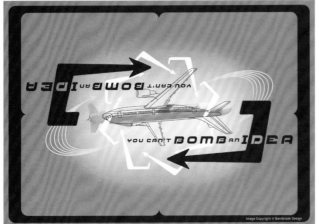

YOU CAN'T BOMB AN IDEA

Image Copyright © Barnbrook Design

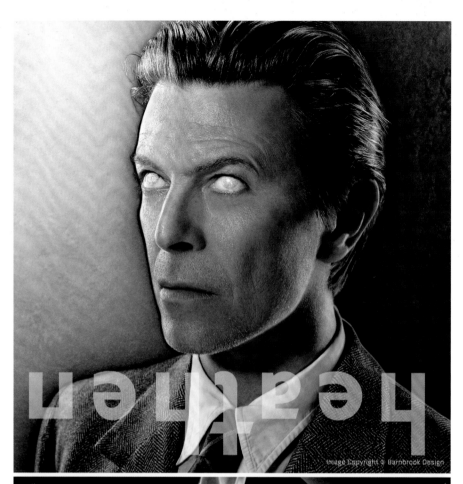

1

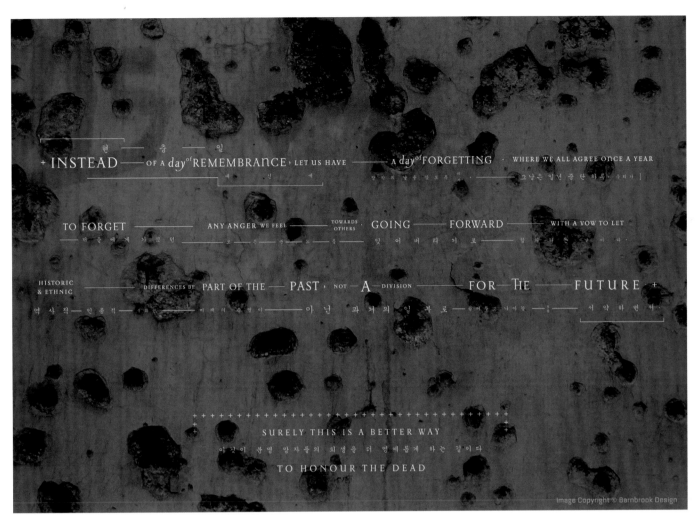

2

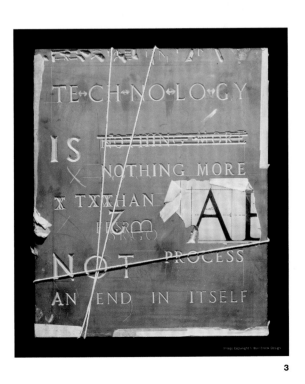

3

1. David Bowie / Heathen / Album / 2002
2. The Day Of Forgetting /
Limited Edition Print /
www.dayofforgetting.com / 2004
3. Technology Is Nothing More Than
A Process Not An End In Itself /
Machine-Carved Stone / 1990

1

2

3

4

5

roppongi hills - kanji characters   six trees   six circles as basic logo

六本木 ヒルズ　　=　　=　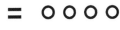　

6

7

1. Daichi Wo Mamoru Kai / Corporate Identity / 2009
2. Daichi Wo Mamoru Kai / Corporate Identity / 2007
3. Shiseido Inoui ID / Identity / Shiseido / 2002
4. I Want To Spend The Rest Of My Life Everywhere,
With Everyone, One To One, Always, Forever, Now /
Damien Hirst Monograph / Book / Booth-Clibborn / 1997
5, 6. Roppongi Hills / Identity / Mori Building / 2003
7. Dignity / Identity / 2007

デザインができること、デザインではできないこと。

──まず、スタジオを始めたきっかけを教えてください。

ロイヤル・カレッジ・オブ・アートを卒業した1990年に、自身のスタジオを設立した。当時の僕は非商業的な作品を追求していたから、誰も僕を雇おうとしなかったし、同時に僕の方でも一般的なグラフィックデザインのプロジェクトに興味を持てなかったね。自分で仕事を選んで、やりたいことに力を注ぎたかった。これが、僕が自分のスタジオを始めた理由。それと、僕がグラフィックデザイナーとして仕事を始めた1990年は、ちょうどデザインの現場にコンピューターが導入されて、デザインを取り巻く環境に大きな変化がもたらされた時期だった。多くのデザイナーは自分で書体を作り始め、実際に素晴らしい作品が生まれていた。かつてそれは多大なお金と労力のかかることだったんだ。そんなふうに、あの時代は、至るところにエネルギーがあふれていた。

スタジオ設立時のフィロソフィー

──スタジオを始めたとき、スタジオとしてのフィロソフィー、デザインに対する哲学のようなものはありましたか?

一番大事なことは、まずサバイヴすること。その次に、意味のないこと、つまらないことに時間を使わないということだった。グラフィックデザイン界には変化が訪れていて、ある一部はどんどんつまらないものになっていった。多くのデザイナーはナイキのような大企業との仕事を求めていたけれど、僕は興味を持てなかった。特にUKでは、デザインが本当に商業的なものになっていたし、大企業を納得させるだけのものになっていたんだ。安易に作られた無益なものを人々に買わせること。そこにはそんな哲学しか見出せなかった。

──そういう風潮は、あなたにとってはつまらないことですよね。

一方で、グラフィックデザインは、政治的、または社会的なテーマをインタラクティヴに伝えることができるツールとして発達してきていた。それに、デザインそのものが一般社会の中で認知が高まってきていたしね。僕としては、こちらの方に興味があったし、これこそが自分のやりたいことだと感じていたよ。

クライアントとデザインスタンス

──あなたのデザインに対するスタンスと、クライアントとの意見が食い違うことはないのですか?

クライアントは、僕たちのデザインスタイルを見て起用したいと思ったから仕事を依頼するわけで、あまりそういう食い違いは起こらない。日本では六本木ヒルズの仕事がよく知られていると思うけれど、あんなふうに商業的なクライアントというのは僕にとって特別なケース。あのときは、僕が手掛けたDamien Hirstの作品集をすごく気に入ってくれて、コンペティションに参加するチャンスを与えてくれた。六本木ヒルズはすごく商業的な施設だし、普段、僕がやっている仕事、スタジオの思想とは少し違う部分からつながった仕事だったね。でも、僕たちが選ばれたのは、彼らがほかの企業にはないようなユニークな考えを持っていたから。だからこそこのプロジェクトをやり通すことができたんだ。

──あなたのデザインを知ったうえで、依頼してくるクライアントが多いということですか?

そうだね。小さなクライアントからは、何か革新性のあるデザインを求められることが多い。やりたい仕事を得るためには、自分たちの作品をプレゼンテーションしていくことが大事だと常々思っている。それから、クライアントと対面すること、人と人とが直接会うことはとても重要だし、お互いを信頼しあうことは私たちがやっているデザインという行為の基本となる部分だと思う。

20年前のデザインシーンと現在

──UKのグラフィックデザインシーンについて聞かせてください。あなたがスタジオを始めた20年前と今ではどんな違いがありますか?

正直に言うと、今のUKグラフィックデザインシーンがどうなっているのか、詳しくは知らない。ただ、昔からポップミュージックとデザインの密接な関わりを感じていて、それらは極めて実験的なポップカルチャーを形成していると思う。革新的なデザイナーやミュージシャンが、革新的な試みを行っている。けれどもその一方で、僕の大嫌いな、大企業と結びついたすごく商業的な面も存在する。それから、20年前と違うのは、教育が大きく変わったことだと思う。昔はお金が掛からなかったけれど、今はきちんとしたグラフィックデザインを学ぶためには多額のお金を払わなければならない。それに、仕事を得ることもますます難しくなっている。でもだからといって、才能のあるデザイナーがいないわけではないし、いいデザイン作品も常に発表されている。そう考えると、UKはグラフィックデザインにとって、すごく健全で真っ当な場所だと思うよ。

デザインそのものに対する評価

──では、今後のUKグラフィックデザインは、どうなっていくと思いますか?

コンピューターの導入によって音楽制作が簡単になったように、デザインも同じ道を辿ると思う。コンピューターへのアクセスが容易になり、ソフトウェアが優れたデザイン作りを後押しするようになるはずさ。けれども、ソフトウェアがアイデアを生み出すわけではないし、デザインはファインアートと同じくらい重要な文化の一分野を担っている。実際、エキシビションを開催するなど、ただデザインを請け負うだけではなく、アーティストとしてのアプローチを実践しているデザイナーも出てきているしね。

デザインにはできないこと

──最後に、デザインの可能性についてお聞きします。あなたのデザイン作品には、メッセージ性の強いものが多いと思うのですが、デザインにできること、できないことについてどう考えていますか？

僕は、あるひとつのグラフィックデザインが、人々の考えを変えることなんてできないと思っている。人に何らかの変化を与えるというのは、そんなに簡単なことではないよ。だけど、人々が何らかのメッセージを得るのを助けてくれる、重要なツールのひとつだと考えているんだ。だから、グラフィックデザインを見て思ったことを議題に、誰かと話し合ってほしい。それが増えれば、その議題は局所的なことではなくメインストリームになるでしょ？　そして願わくば、そこで何らかの変化が起こってほしい。たくさんのグラフィックデザイナーが僕に「ポスターを見て考えを変える人はいるのか？」と聞く。もちろん答えは「ノー」。けれどもグラフィックデザイナーは、常に活発にメッセージを発信し続けるべきだ。なぜなら、それがひとつのデザインアイデアをメインストリームに導くことにつながるし、それは即ち変化の可能性が生まれるということだから。グラフィックデザインはただの広告のプロセスではないし、僕たちは皮肉っぽくあってはいけない。グラフィックデザインはパワフルなツールなんだから。

What Design Can Achieve, And What Design Can't Achieve.

——**Firstly, can you tell me what prompted you to start your studio?**

I set up my studio in the same year I graduated from Royal College of Art in 1990. Back then, I was making work that wasn't commercial and so nobody wanted to hire me, and at the same time I wasn't interested in the graphic design made for mass appeal. I wanted to choose the work myself and put all my efforts in what I wanted to do. This was the reason I started my own studio. Also in 1990 when I became a graphic designer, computers had just been introduced into the workplace and the environment that surrounded design was beginning to change. Many designers started to make their own typefaces and produced some very exciting new work - until then it had been a really an expensive and time-consuming process. It meant there was a lot of energy in design then.

The Initial Philosophy Behind The Studio.

——**When you first set up your studio, did you have a philosophy behind the studio or a certain philosophy towards design?**

The most important thing, firstly was to survive. Secondly, not to spend my own time in boring or meaningless activities. There had been a change in the graphic design industry, and a certain part of it was becoming more and more uninteresting. A lot of other designers were looking to receive work from large companies like Nike, but that didn't interest me. Increasingly in the UK, design was becoming more commercial and the only purpose was to keep the large corporations happy. The philosophy seemed to be to use it make people buy useless stuff that was made in sweatshops.

——**I presume that this trend was not very interesting for you.**

On the other hand, graphic design was developing into a tool that would communicate social or political ideas more interactively. Also design itself was becoming more recognized amongst the general public. For me, this was much more exciting and I began to realize this was what I wanted to do.

The Client And Design Stance.

——**Do you have disagreements between your stance towards design and the client's opinion?**

On the whole, there are rarely such problems as the client is hiring the studio based on the style of design they've seen. People may recognize my work for Roppongi Hills but for me a commercial client like that is quite rare. Mori Buidling Co., Ltd. liked the catalogue I designed for Damien Hirst and offered me a chance to participate in their competition. Roppongi Hills is a commercial venture and it was a job that linked in a slightly different way from the work I do normally and the philosophy of the studio. I do think though because they chose us, they have a unique solution which some other company may not have done for them.

——**So most clients tend to be familiar with your designs when they commission you.**

That's right. From smaller clients we are often requested to produce something innovative, which is great. To do the work you want to do, I think it's important to presenting your own work and communicate directly with the client, I think a good relationship and trust are a fundamental part of what we do in design.

The Design Scene 20 Years Ago And Now.

——**Could you talk about the design scene in the UK? What is the difference between now and 20 years ago when you started out?**

To be honest, I don't really know precisely what's going on in the UK design scene. But I've always felt there is a close link with pop music and design. I think both are seen as forms of experimental pop culture here, meaning that there are innovative designers or musicians working in experimental ways. On the flip side there is the commercial part of design here tightly linked to large corporations which I don't like at all. Another difference now compared to 20 years ago is education. Before it was free, now you have to pay a large fee for formal graphic design training and it's becoming more and more difficult to find jobs. Of course that doesn't mean there aren't any talented designers out there, and you do always see excellent work presented. In that way, maybe the UK is a very healthy place for graphic design.

Assessment Of Design.

——**So, what do you think is going to happen to UK graphic design from here on?**

Music production has become easier with the introduction of the computer, and I think things will follow a similar line in design. More people will have access and the software will help them to do good design. However software is no substitute for good ideas, so I can see design being taken much more seriously as a cultural discipline, as important as fine art. It's already starting to happen as we are often approached as artist to appear in exhibitions rather than just designers.

What Design Can't Achieve.

——**Finally I'd like to ask you about the possibilities of design. There seems to be a strong statement in a lot of your design work but what do you think design can and can't do?**

Personally, I think a single piece of graphic design can't change a person's way of thinking because that's not such an easy thing to do. But, I think it's an important tool in helping people to receive a certain message. So. I'd like a piece of graphic design to become a subject of discussion between people. And the more that happens the subject becomes more mainstream and less marginal right? And ideally I hope some sort of change happens as a result of that. A lot of graphic designers ask me "do you think people change their way of thinking from looking at a poster?". The answer is of course "no". But graphic designers should always actively keep communicating their ideas because they help ideas get into the mainstream which creates the possibility to change. Graphic design isn't only part of the advertising process and we need to stop being cynical. Design is a powerful tool.

JULIA

ジュリア

正直に告白すると、この企画が始まった当初、僕たちはJuliaの存在を知らなかった。それでも今回取り上げることにしたのはMind Design
のHolger Jacobsの強い推薦があったことと、彼らのデザインが持つ〝今〟の感覚に強い魅力を感じたからだ。本書中、最も若いスタジオ
ながら、雑誌『Volt』を手掛けるなど、その実力は折り紙つき。これから先、至るところで彼らの名前を目にするようになるはずだ。

We must honestly confess, that when this project began, we did not know of Julia. However, we decided to focus on them not
only on the recommendation of Holger Jacobs of Mind Design, but because we felt a strong attraction to the "Now" quality in
their design. They are the youngest studio in this publication, but have already proved their strength working on magazines
such as 'Volt'. We expect to see their name everywhere in the future.

2008年、ロイヤル・カレッジ・オブ・アート在学中に出会った3人、イタリア出身のValerio Di Lucente、フランス出身のErwan Lhuissier、ブラジル出身のHugo Timmにより設立。書籍、
ウェブサイト、企業アイデンティティなど幅広い分野で活躍。雑誌『Volt』(Issue 5&6)のアートディレクションのほか、Puma、Nexusなどをクライアントに持つ。

Founded in 2008, Italian Valerio Di Lucente, French Erwan Lhuissier and Brazilian Hugo Timm, met whilst studying at Royal College of Art. Practicing in a wide range of areas from publishing,
websites to corporate identities. Their client list includes Puma and Nexus, as well as art directing 'Volt' magazine(Issue 5&6).

(Left) Erwan Lhuissier / (Center) Valerio Di Lucente / (Right) Hugo Timm

フランスでデザインを学んだErwan、ローマでのグラフィティー経験からタイポグラフィーに興味を持ったValerio、映画と写真の勉強をしてきたHugoと、出自も関心もそれぞれに違う3人。Juliaと名付けたのは、3人の出身地であるフランス、イタリア、ブラジルに共通する短くて覚えやすい名前だったから。どんな仕事も全員で進める彼ら。「非効率になることもあるけれど、3人が違う個性を持っているからこそ話し合って決めることが大切なんだ。大きなテーブルを囲んで仕事をしているから、それぞれが何をしているかわかっているのさ」とErwan。2008年にロイヤル・カレッジ・オブ・アートを卒業したばかりの彼らは、「まだ自分たちのデザインアプローチを探しているところだけど、作品は何か意味を持つべきだという信念は持っているよ」と語る。ビジネスの匂いが薄いこのスタジオは、彼らにとって学校の延長なのかもしれない。仲のよい3人が生み出すデザインは、UKグラフィックシーンに息づく若いパワーを感じさせてくれる。

All three come from different backgrounds and interests, Erwan studied design in France, Valerio found interest in typography through his experience with graffiti in Rome and Hugo studied cinema and photography. They named themselves Julia, as it was a short and easy name to remember commonly found in France, Italy and Brazil. They work together on all their projects. "Sometimes its not so efficient, but it's important to discuss and decide together as we all bring something different. We all work around one large table so we know what one another is up to," says Erwan. The three, who have just graduated from Royal College of Art in 2008, say, "we are still developing our own approach, but we believe that work should have meaning behind it". The studio feels less of a business, and more like an extension to their studies. You sense a youthful energy keeping UK graphic design alive, from the designs of the three close members.

1. Page Tsou / Book
2. The Invisible Dot / Identity (bespoke typeface)

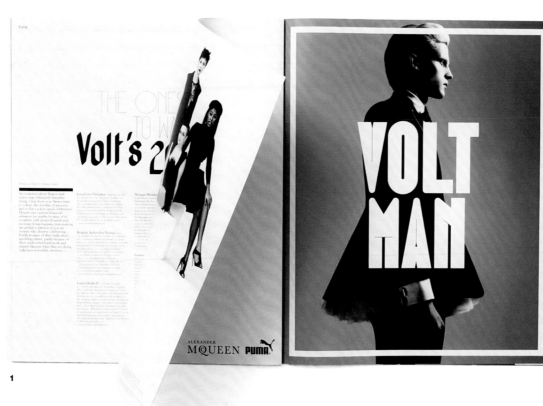

1

1. Volt / Magazine (bespoke typeface)

2. Order / Book / Federico Gallo
3. The Embassy / Catalogue / 20 Hoxton Square
4. Modo / Typeface / Arc Magazine (issue 11)
5. Nexus / Showreel Packaging / Nexus Production

MODO / UNO
MODO / DUE
MODO / TRE
MODO / QUATTRO
MODO / CINQUE

MELVIN GALAPON

メルヴィン・ギャラポン

ダルストン駅から北に約3km。歩いても歩いても住宅街が続き、スタジオらしい建物は一向に見当たらない。それもそのはず、フリーランスで活動するMelvin Galaponは、自宅をスタジオとして使っていたのだから。この小さな空間から生まれるピクセルアートスタイルの作品は、手法の独特さも相まって、脳裏に強い印象を残す。作品について熱心に語る彼のひたむきな姿に、僕たちは強い好感を持った。

Around 3km north from Dalston. We walked and walked through residential streets and found no sign of a studio-like building. Which was not surprising, since Melvin Galapon works free-lance and uses his home as his studio. His work of pixel art style, produced from this small space, combined with his unique technique, leaves a lasting impression. His devoted and passionate attitude in which he spoke about his work left us with a very favorable impression.

2006年、セント・マーチンズ在学中にイラストレーター兼グラフィックデザイナーとしてのキャリアをスタート。イラストレーションとデザインの手法をミックスした作風が高い評価を受け、『The New York Times』『Wallpaper』『The Guardian』など、世界中の新聞、雑誌に作品を提供している。

Began his career as an illustrator/graphic designer while enrolling at St. Martins in 2006. Highly regarded for his style in mixing illustration and graphics, he has contributed to worldwide magazines and newspapers such as 'The New York Times', 'Wallpaper' and 'The Guardian'.

Melvin Galapon

「僕はグラフィックデザインの勉強をしたことがないんだ。大学ではイラストレーションを専攻していたけれど、タイポグラフィーやテクノロジー、SF映画に興味があった。だから、それらを自分の作品に取り入れていったというわけ」。単純な幾何学模様の組み合わせで人の顔や文字を表現するという独特の手法は、主にTVからインスピレーションを受けた。「普段、TVは見ないけれど、TVのピクセル（画素）は僕のデザインに影響を与えていると思う。あと、SF映画もね。特に『Tron』が好きなんだ。最新作品はエレクトロニックミュージックを聴きながら作ったんだよ」。ヴァーチャルワールドにどっぷりつかっているかのように見えるMelvinだが、最近は制作方法が変わってきたと言う。「今まではデジタル機器を使った作品が多かったけれど、ここ2〜3年は手作業がベースになってきた。UKグラフィック全体としても、今後はもっとデジタルとハンドクラフトのブレンドが増えてくると思うよ」。

"I've never studied graphic design before. I was specialized in illustration at university, but I was interested in typography, technology and science-fiction films. So I incorporated these into my work". The inspiration for his unique style of combining simple geometric shapes to create people's faces and letters comes mainly from television. "I don't normally watch television but I think the pixels in the screen have inspired me. And of course SF films, I especially like 'Tron'. My new work was made listening to electronic music". Melvin seems like someone deep in the virtual world but he says his working methods are changing. "Until now I used digital equipment in a lot of my work but for the past 2 or 3 years I've mainly been using hand techniques. I think you will begin to see a blend of digital and hand craft from now on in UK design as a whole".

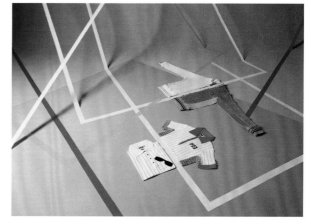

1

2

3

1. Show Off Poster / Limited Edition Record Print / Show Off Records
2. Soundwave / Personal
3. Tape Installation / Wallpaper & Fila

1. Audrey Hepburn Type Portrait / Quotation Magazine
2. Che Guevera Type Portrait / Quotation Magazine
3. Charlie Chaplain Type Portrait / Quotation Magazine
4. Marilyn Munroe Type Portrait / Quotation Magazine
5, 6. Virtual / Personal
7. Feel The Noise / Tshirt Design for Publik Japan
8. Static / Personal
9. Love Is Blind / Personal
10. See No Evil / Printclub Show Screenprint

```
MMMMMMMMMMMMMMMDDMMD$+~=:?=I7I7ZZZOZMDDDOZ?OMMMOOMMMMMMMMMZ      ........................
MMMMMMMMMMMM$$$$7?++====+7I=~+I?Z77$D8D88ZDMZMMMM8DMMMMMMMMZ      ........................
MMMMMMMM8MMD8OI??:::+++?I?+?+7$Z8I$778M$II80$M8MOOMMMMMMMMMZ      ........................
MMMMMMMM$MMMMM8807$$=~=?+?I7II7$Z8?ZZ$MO777IIM?DMZ88MMMMMMMZ      ........................
MMMMMMMMMMMMMMMD08Z07+==?=+~?~+?7OZODMMMM7MO+MOMMMODZMMMMMMMZ     ...................?MDMM
MMMMMMM$MMMMMMMMMMD280Z$Z0$$7$I88D8808N8M$MM880MMMZOMOMMMMMMZ    .............=MMMMMM
MMMMMMM$8MMMMDDDOD80DZ$I+$8880I=?ZMMZZDODZIZ8MMMMMD0=MMMMMMZ     ...............$MMMMMMMM
MMMMMM8ZMMMMMMNM$ZI$ZII$ZOM87MO?IZ7=IDDN$$$MMMMMMMDMIDMMMMZ     ................=MMMMMMMM
MMMMMMMMMMMMMMMMO808M88ZZMOZ7?+II?I?$MM+~7?7DMMMMMMDM7?MMMMZ    .................=MMMMMMMM
MMMMMMMMMMMMM8DMMMMMDDMM80M???$$==7M?+~++~~=MZMMMMMMMOIMMMMZ   ..................+MMMMMMMMM
MMMMMMZMMMMMMMMMM8DMDDDMM?70DMD7ZMMMM8+$8?ZI$DZIMMMMMMM$MMMMMZ ...................DMMMMMMMM
MMMMMMMMMMMMMMMMMMMDD88DMMMMDZMMMMMMMMMMMMOMMMZ?MMMMMMM$MMMMMZ.....................MMMMMMMMMM
MMMMMMMMMMMMMMMMMMMMDMMMMMMMMMORMMMMMMMMMMMDMO7MMMMMDIDMMMMZ   ...................8MMMMMMO,..
MMMMMMMMMMMMMMMMMMMMMMMMMMMMMMHDMMMMMMHDMMMMMMHDMMMMMMO+MMMMZ  ...................OMMMM8:,,..
MMMMMMMMMMMMMMMMMMMMMMMMMMMMMMMDMMMMMMHDONODDDHODMMMMMMM7+IOMMZ ..................MMDOI:,,:..
MMMMMMMMMMMMMMMMMMMMMMMMMMMMMDMM8DOD8MMM8MMMDDODMMMMMMMH+$8MMZ  .................$D807,,:,,.
MMMMMMMMMMMMMMMMMMMMMMMMMMMMMDZMMD8MMMMM8OMMM8ZM8MODMMMMO$ZDMMZ .................MDMM?+808DDD
MMMMMMMMMMMD$ZZMMMMMMMMMMMMMHDMM08MMM$7Z7$M$Z00$ZOMMMZIIDMMZ    .................MMMMM?I7~$MM
MMMMMMMMMMMDZI???+7DMMMMMMMMMODMD8MD87I+=+7$Z$777$ZDMDO7IOMM$   ............,,,ZMMMMMD~=OM8DM
MMMMMMMMMMM807I??++=~=IMMMD8ZOMDN8$7?==?ZODMD8$777$$0$$7I$MM$   ...:I?MMMMMMMNO~~?==::,
MMMMMMMMMMMMM$8MMMO$?+=+=?7+?III+==+$ONMDZ?++?I77II7$$0??8MMZ   .......7,8MMMMMMM=,......
MMMMMMMMMMMMM8Z$$$8MMMMM8I?:===~~~~+$ZZ7$ZMMMMZ$ZIIIII$M7?=DMMZ  ......=Z,7MMMMMMM=,......
MMMMMMMMMMMMMMZ$$7DMMMMZ27I+==~==??IOD8MMM$MMZI+?I7?D=+7MMMZ    ......DMMMMMMMD$:,.......
MMMMMMMMMMMMMD770MMZ7MMMZOI?+===+??$Z=,OD??8I+=++?II?+=I DMMZ   .......:MMMMMMMMO:,......
MMMMMMMMMMMMMMO7I$8$++0=+7???=~=+?=++?77$II?=~=+?IIIO$+$:DMMZ   ......:=MMMMMMMDI:,......
MMMMMMMMMMMMMMD$II?7$77I?+==+=~~+++=+=====~~~~=+?II$0+I7DMMMZ   ......:,:MMMMMMMDD7~,,....
MMMMMMMMMMMMMM$7I?+++++++===++~:+?+==~~~~~::~~++?77$008DDDMMMZ  .......ZDMMMMMMDDOI:,,.+7
MMMMMMMMMMMMMMMM$I?++++====++?~~=++=~~~:~~:~~=+?I778D8DDDMMMZ   .......DMM==MMMMMNMDDI=,,Z?+
MMMMMMMMMMMMMMMM07?++======+??~:=+?+=~~~~~~==+I77$MDD8DMDDMZ    ......=,.,~MMMMNDDDI?=.O:,
MMMMMMMMMMMMMMMM$I?++======+?+~:~+?II===~===+?I77ZMDMDDDDMNMZ   .......DM:+MMMDDDD80=,:,;
MMMMMMMMMMMMMMMMMZI?+++=++??+~:~+??II=====+?I7778D8DDD8DDDZ     .......MMMMMMMDMMDDD8?~~,
MMMMMMMMMMMMMMMMMM$I??++++I??~~=+II7Z=+=++++?I77IDD8DDD88DDZ    ......OO$DMMDMDDDD8D8I$~,
MMMMMMMMMMMMMMMMMMM8$7I??++=+$7?I$$$++++++????III7088D8DD88DZ   ......DMMMMMMMMMMDDMNDDDD
MMMMMMMMMMMMMMMMMMMMO7II???+++=+77==++?I7??+?7II$778D0D888DDZ   ..........=8$MZMMMMMMMMNMM
MMMMMMMMMMMMMMMMMMMMM,.+??I7$$77I+=7ZZ8MOI?????I$Z$78DDDD888DDZ .........O?=,8MMMMMDM8MNM
MMMMMMMMMMMMMMMMMMMMM~,..I+??ZZ$$+.7$0$?++????$ZZZ$I8DD8888DZ   .........OMMMMMMMM7ZM
MMMMMMMMMMMMMMMMMMMMMN=...,?+??$$$$Z7?+++++???$Z0087788888882   ........~Z7=DMMMMMMMMMHM
MMMMMMMMMMMMMMMMMMMMMMN~...,I??++=+====+++?I7$ZZZ7+??=788888DZ  .......?ZZ$$Z??7DMMMMDDDDDM
MMMMMMMMMMMMMMMMMMMMMMMN~...:+I?+==~~~=++?7ZZZZI+++++=?000008Z  :,,,:+?II?77I77I$8000$I$7
MMMMMMMMMMMMMMOOOMMMMN,. .,=7I?+++?7ZZZZZ$+===++?=:70082       :?II=~+?????$?????$Z282$$0
MMMMMMMMMMMMMM?+==~=++7D, .:+~ZZZZZZZZZI===+==+++=$ZZ          +~=?II$000$$7I7+II7I??Z00Z
MMMMMMMMMMMMMMN?=~=++:,,::.  ,,+.=ZZZZ$$$7+===~~~~=~~===+?7Z    I+~~+++$88D0$++++IZZI?I708
MMMMMMMMMMMMMM8I=~=,:=.,::. ..= :Z$$$7I+=~==~~~~~~~:~~==+Z      =+?+=?I+IZ8OZI==+70ZI7?Z$
AUDREY_HEPBURN_M=,~.,,,,:...~.,ZD$?==~~~~:~~:_MELVIN_a_2009    CHE_GUEVERA_?+IZ7$00$I=+?+
```

CHARLIE_CHAPLIN_NNN$~~=Z8N?::~7$====NDNNNNNNNN_MELVIN_ə_2009

MARILYN_MONROE_+++=~~~~~~~~~~~~~~=+NNNNNDZ?++===_MELVIN_ə_2009

1/2/3/4

8

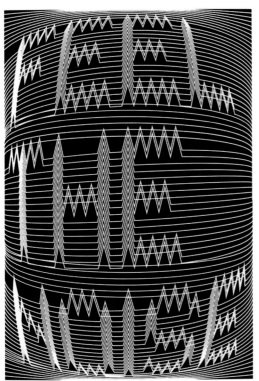

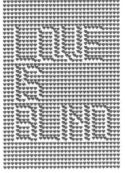

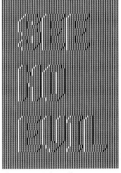

7   **9**   **10**

MICHA WEIDMANN STUDIO

ミカ・ウェイドマン・スタジオ

この企画を進めるにあたって、Micha Weidmannほど誠実に対応してくれたデザイナーはいない。デザインに対しての敏感さと、熱心な姿勢が感じられた。改めて作品を見ると、華やかな雰囲気の中に彼の優しさを見出すことができる。文字は白地の上に置く。見る人の読みやすさを強く意識している作品が多い。残念ながら今回は対面取材が叶わなかったが、機会があれば、ぜひもっと深い話を聞いてみたい。

Micha Weidmann was great to work with on this project, responsive and very enthusiastic about design. Looking at his work, you can see the softness inside his personality. Letters are placed on white. There is care and consideration for the viewer in his work. Unfortunately, we couldn't meet in person but we would love to talk in more depth next time we have the opportunity.

Micha Weidmannにより設立。アートディレクション、デザインはもちろん、ブランドアイデンティティや書籍、雑誌などのコンサルティングなども手掛ける。彼のアートディレクションは Prada、Comme des Garçons、Tate Modern などのブランドにより磨かれてきた。2008年以来、Tokyo Designers Weekのロゴ、出版物のデザインを手掛けている。

Micha Weidmann Studio was founded by Micha Weidmann. He is an art director and designer as well as a consultant for publishers, magazines and identities. His art direction has been honed by brands such as Prada, Comme des Garçons and the Tate Modern. His studio designs the identity and publications of Tokyo Designers Week since 2008.

Micha Weidmann

Micha Weidmannは少年時代のほとんどをスイスで過ごし、14歳のときにデザイナーになることを決意した。「休日、家でダラダラしているのが嫌で近所のデザインスタジオに入り浸っていて、そのデザイナーに強い憧れを抱いたんだ」。彼によると「さまざまなスタイルが混在するUKデザインはコミュニケイティヴでクリエイティヴ。対して、スイスデザインはより分析的で知的」ということだが、スイスの有名グラフィックデザイナー、Josef Müller-Brockmannが考案したグリッド（格子）システムを思い出すと頷ける。スタイリッシュで哲学的とも思えるデザインは、母国の影響を感じさせるし、彼自身も「自分のバックグラウンドはスイスにある」と語る。また、「ディレクションについては、プラダやコム・デ・ギャルソン、テート・モダンでアートディレクターを務めた経験から得たものが多い。それぞれのプロジェクトに最適な形で、単純化し洗練させること、それが僕の手法」とのことで、このあたりからも、スイスデザインの根底にある“分析”をベースにした仕事ぶりがうかがえる。「ロンドンに来たのは、たくさんの文化が集まる街だから。こここそ、自分が求めていた場所なんだ」。

Micha spent most of his childhood in Switzerland where he decided to become a designer at the age of 14. "I was fascinated by a local designer, so instead of sitting around at home I spent my holidays at his studio". According to Micha, "UK graphic design is communicative and creative through the mix of it's many styles and disciplines. Swiss design is more analytical and intellectual." and there is some truth when you think of the Grid system invented by the famous Swiss graphic designer Joseph Müller Brockmann. There is an element of his homeland in his stylish and almost philosophical design, and he states himself that, "My background is in Swiss design but my approach to art direction was defined through working with brands such as Prada, Comme des Garçons and the Tate Modern. My method is to refine and simplify each individual project appropriately". As he claims, you can see that his designs are influenced by "analysis", a basis of Swiss design. "I came to London because of the diverse cultural mix, I love this city, it is what I was looking for".

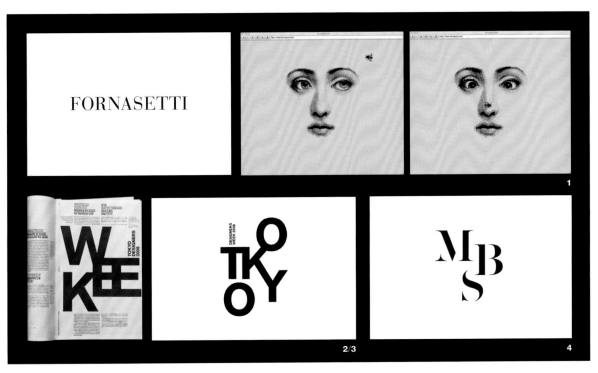

1. Fornasetti / Website / 2010
2, 3. Tokyo Designers Week / Identity and Tabloid Paper / 2008–2010
4. Moira Benigson Executive Search / Identity / 2009

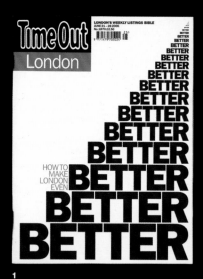

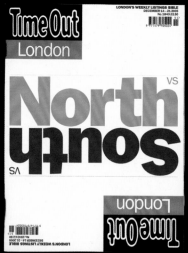

1. Time Out Magazine / Redesign and Art Direction / 2005–2007
2. Louise Bourgeois book / Advertising and Exhibition /
Tate Modern London / 2007
3. Studio Toogood / Identity / 2009–2010
4. New Statesman / Cover Art Direction / 2009–2010
5. The Fashion / Magazine / Art Direction / 2002
6. Swarovski / Magazine / Consultancy / 2004

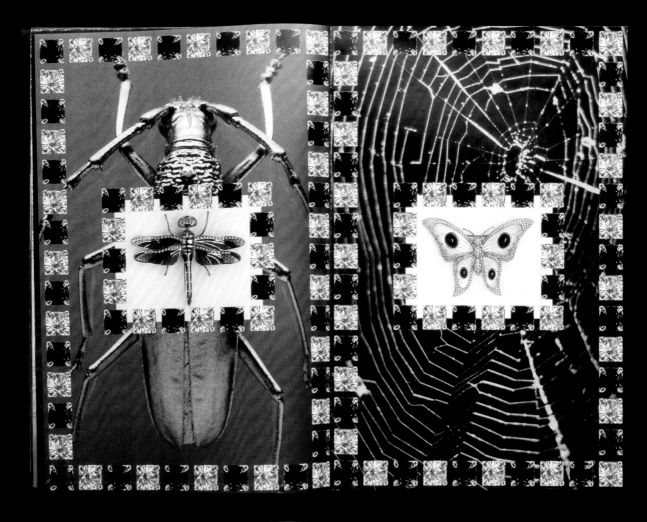

MIND DESIGN

マインド　デザイン

ハックニーエリアを流れる運河沿いにスタジオを構えるMind Design。あちこちに飾られている彼らの作品に交じり、Holger Jacobsの自転車コレクションが並ぶ。かつて日本に住んでいた彼は、僕たちに対してもフレンドリーに接してくれ、取材後にはビールを振る舞ってくれた。スタジオ内を歩き回りながら作品を解説してくれた彼。聞けば聞くほど、考え抜かれたデザインアプローチに、心底、感心させられた。

Mind Design is located by the canal which runs through the London borough of Hackney. The studio space displays past and current work, as well as a generous area reserved for Holger Jacobs' collection of bicycles. Having previously lived in Japan, he made us feel very welcome and even bought us some beers after the interview. He explained his work whilst showing us around the studio. The more we listened to him, the more we were deeply impressed with his well thought out design approach.

1999年、ロイヤル・カレッジ・オブ・アートを卒業したHolger Jacobs により設立。タイポグラフィーや企業アイデンティティに重点を置きながら、書籍、ウェブサイト、インテリア、広告ディスプレイなど、幅広い分野のアートディレクションを手掛ける。Tom Dixon、Artek、Paramount、Tess Management などをクライアントに持つ。

Mind Design was founded by Holger Jacobs in 1999 after graduating from Royal College of Art. Whilst maintaining a strong focus on typography and visual identity, the studio also works in different areas such as publishing, websites, interior and signage. The current client list includes Tom Dixon, Artek, Paramount and Tess Management.

(From Left to Right) Sara Streule, Johannes Höhmann, Holger Jacobs, Craig Sinnamon, Andy Lang

ドイツ出身のHolger Jacobsはロンドンで学んだ後、日本の出版社でアートディレクターとして経験を積んだ。再び英国へ戻った彼は、ひとりで仕事をし始める。その後、アイルランド出身のCraig Sinnamonが加わり、今では5人のデザイナーを擁するスタジオになった。「初めはブックデザインが主だったけれど、そのうちロゴやインテリア、ウェブサイトまで包括的に手掛けるようになったんだ。最近は、レストランやショップ、バーなどのブランディングの仕事がよく来るようになったよ」。自分たちのデザインに、特定のスタイルはないと言うが、「その都度、面白いと思えるものに影響を受けているし、仕事によっても変わる。作品の裏にあるプロセスが僕たちのスタイルと言えるかもしれないね」。Mind Designというスタジオ名は思いつきから生まれた名前。「深い意味があるわけじゃないんだ。言葉遊びが好きで、"mind"には"in"がインしていて面白いなと思って。変えようと思ったときにはもう遅かったんだよね（笑）」。こんなユニークさも彼の持ち味のひとつかもしれない。

Originally from Germany, Holger Jacobs studied in London and went on to work as an art director for a publishing company in Japan. On his return to England he first worked by himself and was later joined by Craig Sinnamon from Ireland. Today the studio is made up of a team of five designers. "At the start it was mainly book design but we managed to expand into different areas, designing logos, interiors, and websites. Recently we are receiving more branding work for bars, shops and restaurants". Holger points out that the work doesn't follow just one particular style "I'm inspired by what is interesting me at that moment, and it depends on each project. You could say the process behind the work is defining our style." The name 'Mind Design' was more a coincidence, "It wasn't meant to sound too clever. I like wordplay and how the word "in" sits inside the word "mind". When I tried to change the name it was too late (laughs)". This humorous side is part of his appeal.

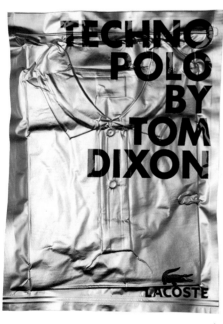

2

1. Lacoste / Eco-Techno Polo Packaging
2. Tom Dixon / Review / 2009
3. Tea / Doily Table Mats

1

2/3

4

1, 2, 3. Circus / Stationery,
Menu Cover Detail, Illuminated Sign
4. Belmacz / Red Catalogue
5. Belmacz / Bauhaus Poster
6. Russell Marsh Casting / Stationery
7. Playlab / Card

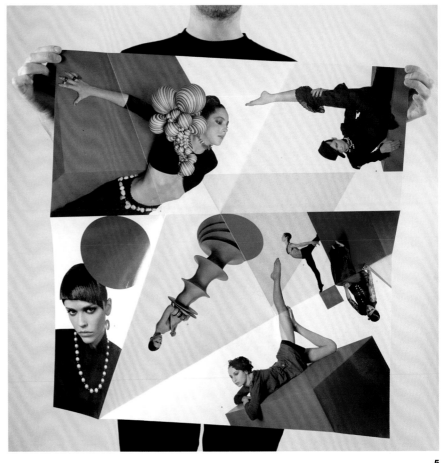

5

7

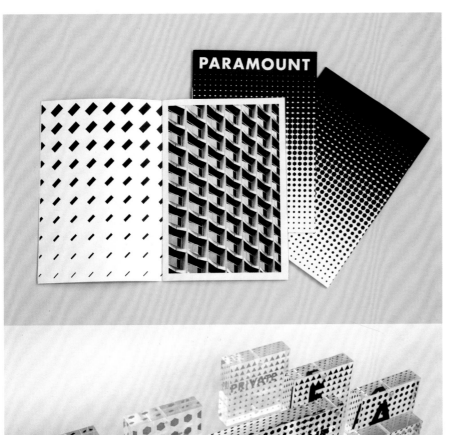

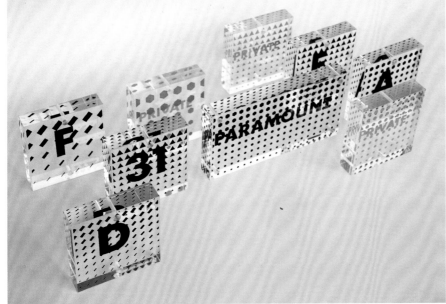

8-11. Paramount / Foyer and Tapestry, Signage,
Sliding Doors (PH_Ed Reeve), Brochure
12. Tess / Model Card Folder, Newspaper
13. Artek / Sausage Chair / Poster

12   13

NEVILLE BRODY

ネヴィル・ブロディ

言わずと知れたグラフィックデザイン界の大御所Neville Brody。彼が立ち上げたResearch Studiosは、今やロンドンだけでなく、パリ、ベルリン、バルセロナにもスタジオを構えている。本書の取材初日、最初のインタビューで少し不安になっていた僕たちに対し、彼はまずリラックスを促し、そして、おそらく日本人であることを考慮してゆっくりとわかりやすく言葉を紡いでくれたのだった。

Neville Brody is, of course, an established figure in graphic design. Research Studios which he founded, now has offices in London, Paris, Berlin and Barcelona. We were a little nervous about our first interview to kick-off the research for this project, but Brody made sure we were relaxed and, taking note that we were Japanese, spoke with great care to make it easier for us to understand him and his concepts.

1980年代、音楽レーベル『Fetish Records』のスリーブデザインや、雑誌『The Face』『Arena』などのアートディレクションを手掛け、世界中の注目を集める。最近の仕事は、BBC、LG Electronics、雑誌『Arena Homme+』など。また、2011年よりロイヤル・カレッジ・オブ・アート、コミュニケーションアート＆デザイン学部長を務める。

Brody achieved worldwide recognition for his sleeve designs for 'Fetish Records' and as art direction for magazines such as 'The Face' and 'Arena'. Recent work includes, projects with the BBC, LG Electronics, and 'Arena Homme+' magazine. He has been appointed as the new Head of Department of Communication Art & Design at Royal College of Art(London) from 2011.

Neville Brody

Research Studios / London 2010

Research Studios / London 2010

Neville Brody's Studio / Research Studios / London 2010

OUR PROCESS

1. RESEARCH.
2. STRATEGY.
3. CREATIVE EXPLORATION.
4. IDEAS.
5. GERMINATION.
6. COMMUNICATION SOLUTIONS.

OUR SMALL & PERFECTLY FORMED

Detail from Research Studios Hallway Project / Research Studios and Harry Malt / London 2010

THE FACE

EIRE 9½p (INC VAT)

HARD TIMES
**WHATEVER HAPPENED
TO THE ZOOT SUIT?**

**Kevin Rowland · Philip K. Dick
La Resistance Graphique
Imagination · Nam June Paik**

NORTHERN SOUL
A primer for the new soul rebels

Photo by Sheila Rock

1

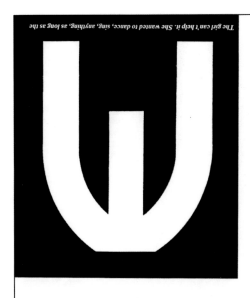

The girl can't help it. She wanted to dance, sing, anything, as long as the

THE FACE
INTERVIEW
INTERVIEW

"I have nothing to say – read my books" is Andy Warhol's standard riposte to most would-be interviewers. David Yarritu – a former assistant of his – and I were hoping Andy would say this to us because we had no intention of mentioning Edie, The Velvet Underground or soup cans, but instead he pushed an apple pie at us and suggested we joined him "working out" after we'd eaten. Andy Warhol – the quintessence of Sixties pop art and the ultimate dinner party guest – has, naturally enough, got into the new American obsession: health, fitness and diet. He has a rigorous exercise routine which he carries out daily in the new 'Factory', a former Con Edison building between 32nd and Madison. As with the old Union Square Factory, he has found another unobtrusive warehouse-type building. Valuable pieces from Andy's private art collection are propped against the walls

as you walk through the white wood corridor from the front of the building (where the *Interview* magazine offices are) to Andy's studio: a vast room which once housed the generators for the plant. One corner of the room is a mini-gym complete with a Yugoslavian physical fitness trainer on hand at all times. More boxes of Andy's belongings are grouped in another corner, with a large crumpled-up Jean-Michel Basquiat painting worth thousands of dollars thrown on top. On the floor are discarded silk screens of Sean Lennon. Two commissioned portraits of a Houston businessman are awaiting collection and a portrait of Jean Cocteau is propped upside down beneath a projector. Inside Andy's studio, it's like a hotel lobby. People wander in and out constantly: a woman puts some tiny galoshes on Andy's pet dog and takes it for a walk, a photographer tiptoes around the

46 THE FACE

THE FACE 47

2

3

4

1. The Face Issue *29* / Cover of Magazine / Hard Times
Times / Wagadon, London 1982
2, 4. The Face / Spreads of Magazine / Hard
Times / Wagadon, London 1981-1986
3. The Face / Various Covers of Magazine /
Times / Wagadon, London 1981-1986

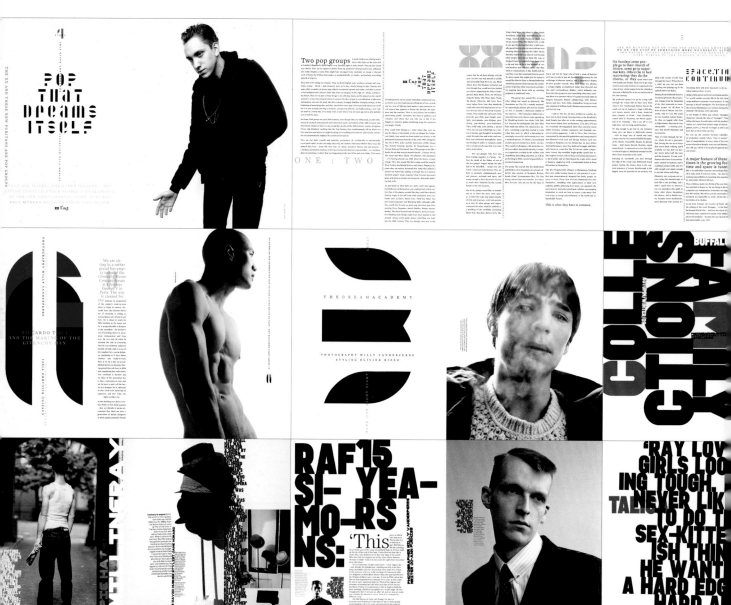

1   2   3   4   5
6   7   8   9   10
11   12   13   14   15

16						17						18

1-7. Arena Homme+ Issue 33 / Spreads of Magazine / Bauer Media / London 2010
8-15. Arena Homme+ Issue 32 / Spreads of Magazine / Bauer Media / London 2010
16. Arena Homme+ Issue 33 / Cover of Magazine / Bauer Media / London 2010
17. Arena Homme+ Issue 32 / Buffalo Cover of Magazine / Bauer Media / London 2010
18. Arena Homme+ Issue 32 / Westwick Cover of Magazine / Bauer Media / London 2010

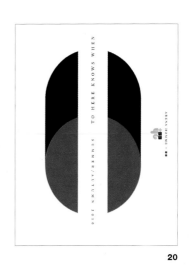

19, 20. Arena Homme + Issue 33 / Spreads of Magazine / Bauer Media / London 2010

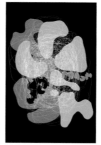

1　2　3　4　5　6

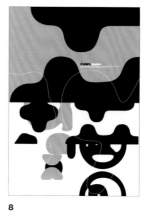

8　9

7

10

1. Make Trouble / Poster / Neville Brody / London 2008
2. Fuse 11 / Pornography / Font and Poster /
FontShop International / Berlin 1994
3. Fuse 15 / Cities / Font and Poster /
FontShop International / Berlin 1995
4. Crash / Font Promotional Poster /
FontShop International / Berlin 1993
5. Fuse 9 / Autotrace / Font and Poster /
FontShop International / Berlin 1994
6. Various Typefaces / FontShop International / Berlin 1982 – 1994
7. Free Me From Freedom / Poster / ROCKET / Tokyo 2009
8. Fuse 15 / Secrets / Font and Poster /
FontShop International / Berlin 2000
9. Fuse 1 / Invention / Font and Poster /
FontShop International / Berlin 1991
10. D&AD Annual / Slipcase and Packaging / London 2009
11. Free Me From Freedom / Poster / Embedded Art / Berlin 2009
12. Brody @ROCKET / Poster / ROCKET / Tokyo 2009

11

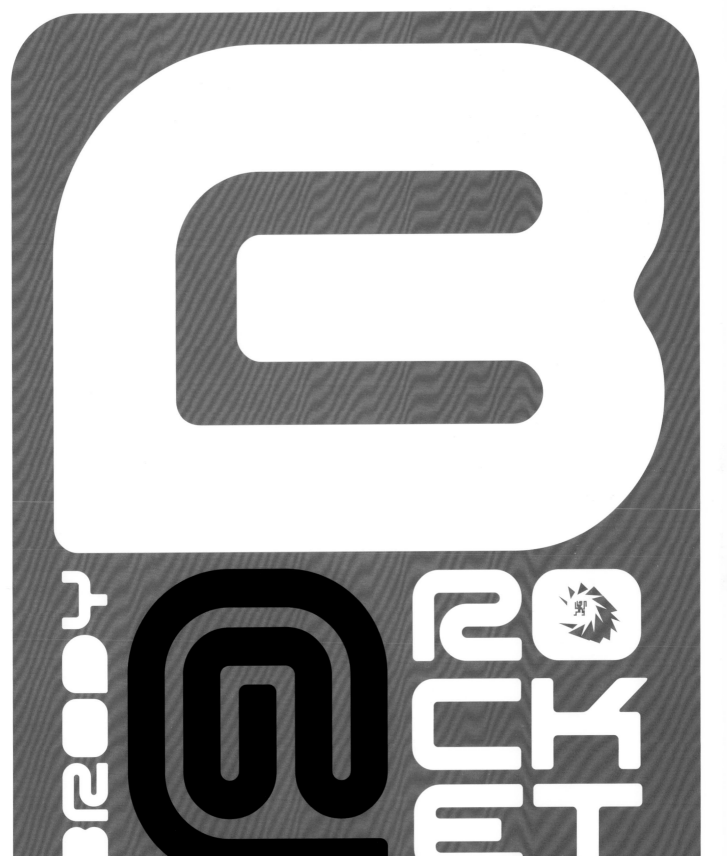

NEVILLE BRODY AT SPACE_ROCKET TOKYO
JANUARY 31 – FEBRUARY 10
TEL/FAX 03 3499 1003 WWW.ROCKET-JP.COM

ロケットでは会場の使用者を募集しています。
使用条件はWWW.ROCKET-JP.COMをご確認の上、
HELLO@ROCKET-JP.COMまでご連絡ください。

ROCKET

グラフィックデザインの30年間と、これから。

——あなたがグラフィックデザインの仕事を始めた1970年代の終わり頃と現在を比較して、デザインを取り巻く環境にどんな違いがありますか?

パンクが始まった1970年代半ば、デザインはとてもインディペンデントで、商業主義とは切り離されたムーヴメントだった。同時にインディペンデントなレコードレーベルやアパレルショップがあり、彼らは若くて無名のデザイナーたちと仕事をしていた。そこにはクリエイティヴな仕事があったし、それを世の中に発信できる環境もあったんだ。そういう状況がなかったら、僕も23EnvelopeもTomatoもThe Designers Republicも、デザインの仕事をしていなかったと思う。でも今は、大きく状況が変わり、音楽もファッションもアートも、すごく商業的なものになってしまった。

——なぜそうなってしまったと思いますか?

パンクやその他のインディペンデントなカルチャーの登場は、大企業にある種の衝撃を与えたと思う。そして、それに対する大企業の反応は、買収とコピー。広告はあらゆるスタイルをコピーしたし、音楽もファッションも新聞も雑誌もそう。結果、ラディカルなもの、刺激的なものはなくなってしまったんだ。なぜなら、コピーコピーコピーで、表現のメインストリームがおしなべて"刺激的"になってしまったからね。

デザインと音楽の良好な関係

——あなたと『Fetish Records』のような関係は、もう過去のものなのでしょうか?

1985年頃に、一部を除いたインディペンデントな音楽レーベルは大企業に買収された。実験的な音楽をやっていたレーベルが姿を消してしまったんだ。Duran DuranやSpandau Balletに代表される、ニュー・ロマンティックでさえも商業的な枠組みに組み込まれてしまったしね。もはや実験的な表現が可能なフィールドは限られてしまい、アンダーグラウンドな音楽シーンは、実験的な作品を作るためによりアンダーグラウンドな方向へ向かっている。昔のようなインディペンデントレーベルは、今は2つ3つしか残っていない気がする。『Warp』ですら、今やすごく商業的になっちゃったしね。

レコードスリーブからタイポグラフィーへ

——グラフィックデザインと音楽が良好な関係を保っていたのは、いつ頃までぐらいでしょうか?

Jonathan BarnbrookやWhy Not Associatesが出てきた1980年代後半頃には、グラフィックデザインと音楽の結びつきはすでに終わりを迎えていたと思う。ちょうどその頃コンピューターが登場して、デザイナーたちがタイポグラフィーの分野で実験的な制作を始めた。Jonathan Barnbrookなどのデザイナーが、コンピューターを使って、どんどん新しい書体を生み出していたよね。かつてはレコードスリーブというフィールドで実験的なデザインが盛んに行われていたけれど、彼らの実験の場がレコードスリーブからタイポグラフィーへと移っていったんだ。

——今後、音楽業界においてグラフィックデザインはどんな役割を担うと思いますか?

音楽業界について言えば、新しい発想は、ヴィジュアルではなく技術的なエンジニアリングの分野から出てくると思う。なぜなら音楽は、ものとしての実体がなくなってしまったから。1980年代はレコードスリーブがあって、次にCDジャケットがあって、今はMP3。MySpaceもあるけれど、ページデザインは最悪だ。グラフィックデザインが活かされる場がどんどん少なくなっている。

2010年、デザインが置かれている状況

——去年からまた『Arena Homme+』で、雑誌のアートディレクションを手掛けていますね。

最初はあまり乗り気ではなかったけれど、始めたらすごく楽しくなった。『Actual』以来、15年ぶりに雑誌をデザインしている。実験的な作品が次々と発表されている雑誌というフィールドでも、一部を除いてはすごく保守的だったりする。例えば、1981年に僕たちが『The Face』を始めたときも、まわりの雑誌はすごく伝統的なスタイルで作られていた。当時、雑誌カルチャーに関わっていた人たちにとって、『The Face』の登場は衝撃的だったはず。

——雑誌を取り巻く状況をどう考えていますか?

雑誌メディアだけじゃなく、ここ25年間、あらゆる文化は停滞していて、本当に新しいものは生まれていない。1985年以降、デザインもただの商品に成り下がってしまい、それはカルチャーと呼べるものではなくなってしまった。ノスタルジックに昔の文化を懐かしむ人も多いけれど、僕は2010年が転機になると思っている。銀行システムが破綻して経済的に大きな変化が訪れている今、デザインが再びカルチャーになれるチャンスだと感じているんだ。

UKグラフィックデザインの今後

――では、今後のUKグラフィックデザインは、どうなっていくと思いますか?

約20年間、デザイン業界の中心にいるデザイナーは大きく変わっていない。たくさんの若いデザイナーが出てきたけれど、注目すべきデザイナーは本当に一握りじゃないかな。多分、日本でも状況は同じでしょう? 革新的なデザイン作品を発表しているデザインスタジオは数少ないし、田中一光以来、新しい領域を切り開く指導者のようなデザイナーも出てきていないように見える。

――けれども、まったく新しい才能が生まれていないわけではないと思います。

若くて実験的なデザイナーはたくさんいる。けれども、彼らには発表する機会がないんだ。2010年9月に『Anti-Design Festival』というイベントを開催するんだけれど、そこには非商業的で刺激的なグラフィックや実験的なフィルム、バッドな家具に奇抜なファッションなど、急進的な作品が集まると思うよ。

デザインと共にカルチャーを作る存在

――どこかに優秀な若手デザイナーが活躍できるフィールドはないのでしょうか?

あらゆる産業が商業的になりすぎて、デザインをサポートする存在が見あたらない中で、もしかしたら、インターネットが唯一残されたフィールドかもしれない。けれども今はまだ、グラフィックデザインにとってよい仕事場とは言えないよね。今、インターネットの中でグラフィックデザインを手掛けているのはエンジニアであって、彼らは優れたグラフィックデザイナーではない。現在、グラフィックデザインに与えられるプロジェクトは本当に小さくなったし、インディペンデントなものは商業的なプロジェクトとは相容れない状況にある。すごく難しい時代だよ。かつての音楽業界のように、デザイナーをサポートしながら、一緒になってカルチャーを形成していくような業界が必要だ。そういう関係があれば、もっと面白くなるし、そうなってほしいと思っているんだけどね。

Detail from Research Studios Hallway Project / Research Studios and Harry Malt / London 2010

30 Years Of Graphic Design And The Future.

——**What are the differences in the environment surrounding design between now and when you first started out as a graphic designer in the late 1970's?**

In the mid 1970's punk arrived and design was very independent, a movement far removed from the corporate industry. At the same time, there were independent record labels and fashion boutiques who worked with young and unknown designers. There was creative work being produced and also a platform to distribute it to the world. If there wasn't this situation, I don't think myself, 23 Envelope, Tomato or The Designers Republic would have been involved in design. But now its different isn't it. Music, fashion and art have all become commercialized.

——**Why do you think that happened?**

I think the emergence of punk and other independent cultures gave a certain shock to the larger corporation. And their reaction in return was to buy out and copy it. Advertising copied all the different styles, and the same for music, fashion, newspapers and magazines. The result is that anything radical or stimulating has gone. Because its all copy, copy, copy and now the mainstream describes itself as "radical" across the board.

The Positive Relationship Between Music And Design.

——**Do you think something like your relationship to 'Fetish Records' is something of the past?**

In and around 1985, most of the independent record labels were purchased by large corporations, apart from a small handful, even new romantic acts headed by Duran Duran or Spandau Ballet became part of this commercialized industry. Now there are a few areas where you can be experimental, underground music for example is heading even more underground to be able to make experimental work. Now I think there are only 2 or 3 independent labels like the past. Even 'Warp' Records are now really commercial.

From Record Sleeves To Typography.

——**When do you think this positive relationship between music and graphic design ended?**

When Jonathan Barnbrook and Why Not Associates appeared in the late 1980's this relationship was already coming to an end. By this time the computer had arrived, and designers started to experiment more with typography. The record sleeve was the field designers experimented in, but that shifted to typography.

——**In the future what role do you think graphic design will play in the music industry?**

In regard to the music industry, I think new ideas will emerge not from the visual but from the technological engineering field. Because now, there's no physical product in music anymore. In the 1980's there were record sleeves, then CD covers and now MP3. There's Myspace, but the page design is awful. There's less and less opportunity to make use of graphic design.

The Situation Of Design In 2010.

——**From last year, you've started to work as the art director for 'Arena Homme+'.**

At first I wasn't so keen, but now that I've started it's great. Since working on 'Actual', it's been 15 years since I designed a magazine. Even in an industry like magazine publishing where a lot of experiment work appears, apart from a small section it's very conservative. For example, when we first started 'The Face' in 1981, the style of most other magazines was traditional. I think the appearance of 'The Face' must have been quite shocking.

——**What is your point of view on the current situation of the magazine industry?**

In the past 25 years nothing really new has appeared, not just in the magazine industry, but culture in general has been at a stand still. Design has just become a commodity and it became something you can't call culture. There are a lot of people who like to feel nostalgia for the past but I think 2010 may be a turning point. There's a huge change in finance with the collapse of the banking system and I think design may have a chance to become culture again.

The Future Of UK Graphic Design.

──**How do you see the future development of UK graphic design?**

For around 20 years, the main designers in the center of the design industry were the same. There are many young designers but only a few who seem interesting. Isn't it the same in Japan? There are only a few design studios producing great work, and after Ikko Tanaka there doesn't seem to be any other influential designer leading the field.

──**However, there are still new talent appearing.**

Yes, there are plenty of young and experimental designers. But there isn't really a platform for them to showcase. In September 2010 we are hosting an event called 'Anti-Design Festival', and there we're hoping to show a collection of radical work like uncommercial graphics, experimental film, bad furniture and alternative fashion.

Cultivating Culture As Well As Design.

──**What field do you think young and talented designers would be able to flourish in?**

In an age where all industries are now commercialized and there is a lack of support for design, the Internet may be the only environment left. But I also don't think you can call the Internet a great working platform for graphic designers. Engineers are dealing with graphic design in the Internet but they are not great designers. The size of projects given to graphic designers has really shrunk, and in the current situation, independent projects conflict with commercial projects. It's a really difficult time. Like the music industry of the past, we need an industry where culture is built up together, supporting the designers. Things would be much more interesting if these relationships appeared, it's what I'm hoping for.

NON-FORMAT

ノン・フォーマット

本書の中で、唯一ロンドンにスタジオを構えていないNon-Format。元々はロンドンに拠点を置いていたものの、今は国外に住まいを移している。TDC賞を受賞するなど日本での知名度が高いのに加えて、本書の参加デザイナーから評価する声も多い。デザイナーから推薦されるデザイナー。きっと今後も革新的な作品を生み出し続けるに違いない。なぜなら、同業者ほど厳しい目を持つ存在はないのだから。

Non-Format is the only studio in this publication who are not based in London. They were, previously, but are now located overseas. They are well known in Japan winning two TDC awards, but also all the other participating designers regard them very highly indeed. They are designers recommended by designers. We are sure they will continue producing innovative design in the future. That is because there is no one more critical than colleagues in the same trade.

2000年、イギリス出身のJon Forssとノルウェー出身のKjell Ekhornにより設立。現在は、アメリカ ミネアポリスとノルウェー オスロの2カ所に拠点を置く。音楽、アート、ファッション、広告など幅広い分野でアートディレクションとデザイン、イラストレーションを手掛ける。2006年、2008年にはTOKYO TDCの一般部門にてTDC賞を受賞。

Founded in 2000 by British Jon Forss and Norwegian Kjell Erkhorn. Currently based separately in Minneapolis, USA and Oslo, Norway. They work in design, illustration and art direction for clients in various fields such as art, music, fashion and advertising. Awarded the TDC Prizes 2006 and 2008 by TOKYO TDC.

(Top) Kjell Ekhorn / (Bottom) Jon Forss

Non-FormatのJon ForssとKjell EkhornはUKで知り合ったものの、現在Jonはアメリカに、Kjellはノルウェーに住んでいる。Kjellによると「Skypeやメールを上手く使っている」そう。Jonが寝る前にその日の進捗状況をメールで送り、Kjellが起きて続きを進めるといった具合で、仕事は意外とスムーズに進む。情報化社会となった現代ならではのスタイルだ。2人は1999年に共通の知人を通して知り合い、音楽雑誌『The Wire』から2人にアートディレクションの依頼があったことをきっかけに、スタジオを設立。Jonは「自分がキャリアをスタートした1989年には、オフィスにコンピューターがなかったんだ。技術よりも感覚やアイデアを重視するスタイルが身についたのはその頃かな。コンピューターを使うようになった今でもそれは変わらない」と語る。デジタルを最大限に活用しながらも、できあがってくる作品がどこか人間臭くユーモラスなのは、こういった背景によるのかもしれない。

Non-Format's Kjell Ekhorn and Jon Forss met in the UK, but currently Jon lives in USA and Kjell in Norway. According to Kjell, "We are using Skype and e-mails very well". It all works surprisingly smoothly; Jon sends his progress situation by email before going to bed, and Kjell wakes up to continue the work. The two met through friends in 1999, and set up their studio when they were offered work by the music magazine 'The Wire'. "When I started my career in 1989, I didn't have a computer in the office. I think that was when I acquired a style of focusing more on my senses and ideas rather than technique. I use a computer now but that hasn't changed"(Jon). Even when they fully make use of digital technology, they produce work which is somehow human and humorous, and that may be due to their backgrounds.

1. Non-Format Love Song / Complete Book Design / Die Gestalten Verlag / 2007
2. The Chap – Ham / CD Packaging / Lo Recordings / 2005
3. Barry 7's Connectors / LP Packaging / Lo Recordings / 2001

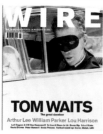

1

2

3

1. The Wire / Art Direction & Design / 2001-2005

2. The Economist / Poster Campaign / Typographic Illustrations /
AMV BBDO / 2007 & 2008

3. IBM Supply Chain / Print Advertisement / Illustration /
Ogilvy & Mather / 2009

4. Varoom / Art Direction & Design /
The Association Of Illustrators / 2006-2009

5. I Did Mediocre Stuff While You Were Still At School /
Hand Drawn Poster / Letraset / 2006

6. Jean-Jacques Perry & Luke Vibert Present Moog Acid /
CD Packaging / Lo Recordings / 2007

7. Shakalakka / Billboard Advertisement for LG / BBH / 2008

8. Endless Endless / Fashion Story Created in Collaboration with
Photographer Jake Walters / Cent Magazine / 2008

9. The Chap – Mega Breakfast / CD Packaging / Lo Recordings / 2008

10. Greg Lynn Form / Book / Rizzoli / 2008

11. Back To Black / LP Packaging / Whitechapel Art Gallery / 2005

12. LoAF / Music Packaging Series / LoAF / 2006-2007

4

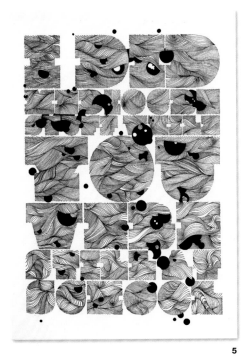

5

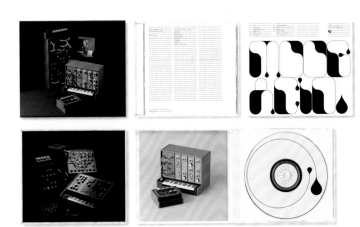

6

7

8

9

10

11

12

OWEN GILDERSLEEVE

オーウェン・ギルダースリーブ

Owen Gildersleeveは、クリエイターの仲間と一軒家をシェアしてEvening Tweedというグループを結成している。ベッドの隣に置かれた2つのデスクが彼のワークスペースだ。ひとつにはMacが置かれ、もうひとつはハンドクラフトを大事にする彼の作業机。ガーリーな印象の強い作風だが、その一言では括れない奥深さも持つ。日々デザインの手法をも模索する彼には、発展途上という言葉がよく似合う。

Owen Gildersleeve shares a house with other creators and is part of a group, Evening Tweed. The two desks next to his bed are his work space. A Mac on one, and the other a work desk for his important hand craft. His style may give a slightly lovely impression, but he has a deepness that can't be summarized by one word. For someone who searches daily for new methods, the expression, on a developing curve, seems to fit him well.

2008年、ブライトン大学を卒業すると同時にデザイナー兼イラストレーターとしてのキャリアをスタート。3Dのクリエイションを平面に落とし込む手法と、常に新しい素材、技術を取り入れるスタンスで制作を続ける。また、若手ながら、『The Guardian』『iD Magazine』『The New York Times』などの新聞、雑誌に作品を提供している。

Starts his career as a designer/illustrator after graduating from Brighton University in 2008. His style is based in continually incorporating new techniques and materials, and explores a method of translating 3D creations into 2D. At his young age, he is already contributing to newspapers and magazines such as, 'The Guardian', 'iD Magazine' and 'The New York Times'.

Owen Gildersleeve

2008年の大学卒業後、『The New York Times』で発表したタイポグラフィー作品を皮切りに、着実にキャリアを積み重ねてきた Owen。紙を切り抜いて作る立体的なタイポグラフィーやクロスステッチをモチーフにした、どこかノスタルジックで温かみのある作品の多くは手作業によるものだ。「例えば、ペーパーカットワーク。最初はどんなものになるのか正確にはわからないけれど、手を動かしていくうちにどんどん形になってくる。それがとても楽しいんだ。でも、デジタルで作業することもあるよ。仕上がりが正確にわかるのも、ときにはいいからね」。大学で写真とグラフィックデザインを学んだ彼は、ファインアートを意識した作品を心掛けているという。その一方で、ドゥームメタルのバンドでドラムを叩くというハードな一面も。いわく「音楽活動は、ややこしいペーパーカットワークの合間の気分転換になっているんだ」。彼の作品に見られる溶けかけの文字や、触ると痛そうなギザギザの文字にはこういったバックグラウンドが反映されているのかもしれない。

After his graduation from university in 2008, Owen used his typography work presented in the 'The New York Times' as a spring board to steadily build up his career. Much of his work is hand crafted work, such as his stereoscopic typography made by cut up paper or cross stitch inspired pieces, have an air of warmth and nostalgia about them. "For example, the paper cut pieces. At first you're not exactly sure how they are going to end up, but as your crafting them they start to take shape. That's what's fun about them. I also work using digital equipment. Pieces that you know exactly how they finish, are sometimes nice too". He studied photography and graphic design but says he is more conscious of fine art in his work. On top of that he also plays drums for a doom metal band. He claims, "My musical outlet helps keep me sane during all the intricate papercut projects". Whether they look like they are melting or jagged and painful to touch, the letters that feature in his work may be a reflection of his background.

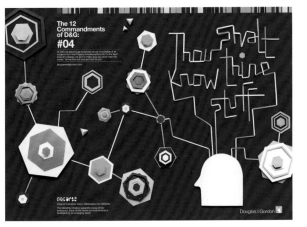

1.

1. Thou Shalt Know Thine Stuff / Douglas & Gordon
2. Motive Sounds / Motive Sounds Recordings
3. If In Doubt Thou Shalt Do the Right Thing / Douglas & Gordon

3

1

2

3

1. Cutting Taxes / Money Magazine
2. The Recession (part 1) / iD Magazine
3. The Recession (part 2) / iD Magazine

5

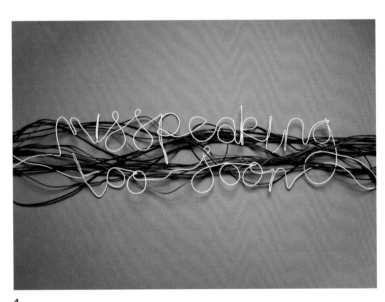

4

6

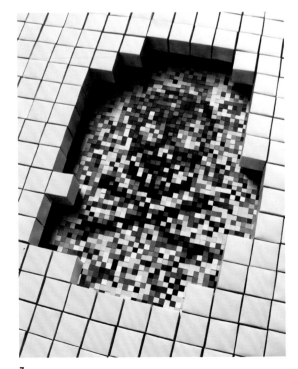

7

4. Misspeaking Too Soon / The New York Times
5. Eye Bird / Nobrow
6. November / Minale Design Strategy
7. Video Game Piracy / Wired

9

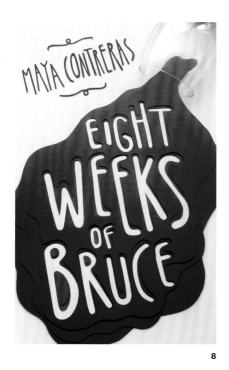

8

8. Eight Weeks of Bruce / Maya Contreras
9. Winter Sweater / Fast Company Magazine
10. Back Too School / Fast Company Magazine
11. Hidden Depths / The TATE
12. Seas of Infinity / Engrave Your Book
13. You'll Laugh and Cry / The Guardian

10

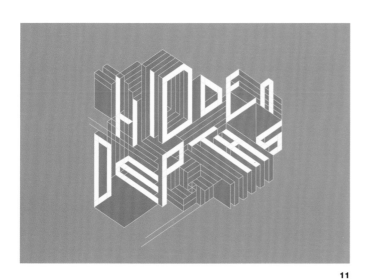

11

12

13

STUDIO MYERSCOUGH

スタジオ・マイヤスコフ

オールド・ストリートエリアにあるホクストン・スクエア、Morag Myerscoughは、そのすぐ側にスタジオを構えている。日本ではあまり知られた名前ではないが、UKでは広く注目を集めるデザイナーのひとりだ。明るくおおらかな人柄は、彼女が生み出すカラフルでポップな作品イメージそのまま。取材当日は体調がすぐれないにもかかわらず、活発な愛犬Lemmyと一緒に、僕たちを歓迎してくれた。

Morag Myerscough's studio is located near the Old Street, Hoxton area. She is maybe less known in Japan, but in the UK, she is counted as one of the most influential designers. She has a cheerful and laid-back personality, and gives a similar impression to her colourful and pop-like work. She was not feeling well on the day of the interview, but welcomed us with open arms with her little animated Lemmy.

セント・マーチンズを卒業後、ロイヤル・カレッジ・オブ・アートにて修士課程を修了したMorag Myerscoughにより、1993年に設立。アートディレクション、デザインはもちろん、商業施設、エキシビションなどの空間デザインも手掛ける。主な仕事に、Design Museum『Formula One』、Royal College of Art『Great Exhibition』などがある。

Founded in 1993 by Morag Myerscough after graduating from St. Martins and on completion of her Masters' at Royal College of Art. As well as art direction and design, she works as a spatial designer in exhibitions and commercial institutions. Her body of work includes, 'Formula One' at Design Museum and 'Great Exhibition' at Royal College of Art.

Morag and Lemmy in her living room

Lemmy

1

1. Westminster Academy, London / Hand-Painted Lettering / 2007
2. Alan Aldridge: The Man with Kaleidoscope Eyes / Design Museum / 2008

1

2

3

4

1. London College of Communication (LCC) / Building Signage and Directory / 2009
2, 3. Art-Tea - Tea Building, Shoreditch / Visuals for Installation Over 7 Floors in the Building / Currently Being Happening / 2010
4. London Born London Bred… / Part of a Series of Posters by a Group of Chosen Designers 'London Posters' at the London Design Festival / 2009
5. The Deptford Project / Creation of Interior and Exterior Completed / 2008 / Handmade Furniture from Recycled Materials / Handpainted Exteriors, using Hand-Cut Stencils / Recycled Song Lyrics and Phrases / Elvis Shoe Loo — by Artist Luke Morgan / (Morag and Luke Proudly Showing Their Stools)

1. The GREAT Exhibition / RCA Summer Shows /
Digital Font Hand-Built and Designed for the Project, Digitally
Printed Text on Ply. (Contrast Between Nature and Technology) /
2007
2. The Mayor's Great Spaces / Trying Out Fonts, Studio Wall / 2009

人と空間の関係をデザインする。

──グラフィックデザインを始めたきっかけを教えてください。
1980年代前半に、セント・マーチンズで初めてグラフィックデザインを学んだけれど、当時のグラフィックデザインは、1960年代にあった多領域を横断する幅広いアプローチを失い、パッケージ、冊子などの印刷物、広告など、それぞれの領域に細分化したものになっていた。例えば、ハンカチの箱やオレンジジュースの容器など、外側だけのデザインにうんざりしていた私は、大学2年目にして、このままグラフィックデザインを続けていくかどうか迷っていたの。

──では、なぜグラフィックデザイナーの道を選ぶことになったのでしょうか?
学部長だったGeoff Fowleの存在が、グラフィックデザインに対する考え方を変えるきっかけになったわ。大学での最後の年、「グラフィックデザイナーとしてやりたいことがあるなら、制限を受ける必要はないし、ときにはルールを破ってでもやりたいことをやるべきだ」と彼は教えてくれた。そして「中途半端な目標を設定してはいけない。たとえ達成する自信がなくても、考えうる限り高いところに目標を設定すべきだ」とも。私は、自分のキャリアのすべてを通して、この言葉を実践してきたわ。

セント・マーチンズ時代に学んだこと

──大学時代の経験は、今のあなたのスタイルに影響を与えていますか?
セント・マーチンズで学んだことはたくさんあるけれど、そのすべてが自分のデザインアプローチにぴったり合うものではなかったわ。私の母はテキスタイルデザイナーで、父はミュージシャン。だから幼い頃からずっと、カラフルな布と美しいビオラの音色に囲まれて仕事をしている両親の姿を見て育ってきた。そんな環境だったからか、私はたくさんの色を使うデザインが好きだったけれど、当時流行っていたのは色を限定したヴィジュアル。Neville Brodyなどの影響がすごく強かったんだと思う。だから私は、グラフィックデザイナーの作品を意図的に見ないようにして、その代わりにAndy WarholやRichard Hamilton、Eduardo Paolozziなどのポップアート作品とイタリアのデザイン集団Memphisの作品ばかりを見ていたわ。

セント・マーチンズからRCAへ

──セント・マーチンズを卒業後、ロイヤル・カレッジ・オブ・アート(RCA)に進んだんですよね?
RCAでは、タイポグラフィーとイメージが別々に存在するのではなく、2つを統合するデザインに夢中になっていたの。卒業する頃には、大学側から「あなたのデザインアプローチでは、就職は難しいかもしれない」なんて言われたりもしたけどね。でもすぐにラム&シャーレイというデザイン会社が、『Next Directory』という女性ファッション誌の仕事を依頼してくれて、1988年から約1年間、表紙と巻頭ページのデザインを担当することができた。当時の『Next Directory』は約300万部を売り上げる人気雑誌で、さまざまな企画に関わることができたし、本当に楽しくてすごく勉強になったわ。

──あなたにとって、デザイナーとして初めての仕事がトラディショナルな印刷物のデザインだったのは、意外なことに思えます。
最近は、大学を卒業してすぐに個人で仕事を始めるのが当たり前のようになったけれど、当時はまだまだ稀なこと。すごくラッキーだったと思う。その後、私はイタリアへ渡ることを決めた。ミラノでは、プロダクトデザイン界の巨匠Michele De Lucchiの元で働き、その後Alessandro Mendiniの依頼でSwatchのデザインも手掛けたわ。帰国後、デザイナーのJane Chipchaseとスタジオを設立したけれど、経済不況の影響で上手くいかなくなって解散。結局1993年、自分ひとりでこのスタジオを設立するに至ったの。

ポップアートの影響

──今までのキャリアを振り返って、一番影響を受けたものは何でしょう?
先日、講義をする機会があって、そのときに会った教育者でイラストレーターのLawrence Zeegenが、私の作品を見て「すごくポップアートの影響が強い」と評してくれた。それまで一度もそんなふうに直接的な影響があると感じたことはなかったけれど、家に帰って部屋に飾ってあるAndy WarholやBridget Riley、Banksy、Jamie Reid、Milton Glaser、Pure Evilなどの作品を見ていたら、学生時代に好きだった作品を思い出し、そしてそれは今でも変わっていないと感じたの。彼の見解はすごく的を射ていると思った。というのも、彼らの作品を見ていて、創作のエネルギーを瞬発的に爆発させたような作品が好きで、こじつけを重ねたようなものは好きじゃないと気づいたから。私も長い時間をかけてアイデアを練るけど、考えがまとまったら一気に作り上げる。そういうスタイルでいつも制作してきた。

独特の制作プロセス

——具体的にどのようなプロセスでプロジェクトを進めているのか、教えてください。

まず、クライアントや関係者との綿密なミーティングを持つことが、大事な要素のひとつ。文章だけのやりとりでは、そのプロジェクトに対する理解が限定されてしまうけれど、対面すれば率直な質問を投げかけられるし、その答えも得られるでしょう？　私は、アイデアを出す前にじっくり考えるタイプだから、対面するというプロセスがすごく重要。そしてそのプロジェクトについて熟考した後でリサーチし、得られた情報で自分の頭を刺激する。すると、いくつかのアイデアが生まれてくるのね。手描きのスケッチだったり立体的なモデルだったり、アウトプットの形はさまざまだけれど、テーブルの周りにありとあらゆる要素をピンで留めて、さらにアイデアを発展させていく。考えに考えを重ねることで自分のアイデアに自信が持てるようになり、自信があれば説得力のあるプレゼンテーションができる。自分のアイデアを信じていれば、相手も同じように信じてくれる。私は、お互いの信頼が最も大切なことだと思っているわ。

"プレイス・メイキング"

——客観的に見て、あなたのデザインにはどのような特徴があると思いますか？

今現在、私は自分のことを純粋なグラフィックデザイナーだとは思っていないの。グラフィックデザイナーという意味では、私よりも優れた人が周りにたくさんいる。例えば、ある建物の内観グラフィックデザインを手掛けていたとして、そのとき、もし家具も自分でデザインした方がいいと思えば、迷わずそれも手掛けるわ。空間と人がどのように呼応するのかを考えながらね。私は常にそういうスタンスでプロジェクトに向き合っている。先日、ある建築家が私のやっていることを、"プレイス・メイキング"と言ったけれど、今の私にとって、それがすごく適当な表現だと思う。グラフィックデザインをテーマにしたこの企画に、波風を立てたいわけではないけどね（笑）。

Designing The Relationship Between The Space And Human Being.

——**What was the reason you started graphic design?**

I first studied graphic design at St. Martins in the early 1980's, but the graphic design at the time had lost its multi-disciplinary approach of the 1960's and had become divided into packaging, print, advertising and so on. I was fed up with designing the outside of a hankie box and an orange juice carton, and already in my second year not sure whether I wanted to continue with graphic design.

——**So how did you end up choosing the path of a graphic designer?**

In my final year Geoff Fowle was my head of department and main tutor, and he was the reason I changed my perspective on graphic design. He taught us that, "As a graphic designer you don't need to be restricted, if there is something you want to do, you should at times break the rules," and to, "never aim in the middle, always aim for the highest level even if your unsure you can achieve it". All throughout my career, I have practiced those words.

Experiences Learnt At College.

——**Did your experience at college influence the style of your work?**

There are many things I learnt at college, but not everything suited my approach completely. My mother is a textile designer and my father a musician. So I grew up seeing my parents working, surrounded by colorful textiles and the beautiful sound of the viola. I loved designs with lots of different colors, but the order of the day was visuals with limited colors. I thought everybody was very much influenced by the work of Neville Brody. So I made a point of trying to avoid looking at work by graphic designers, and instead looked at works by Pop artists like Andy Warhol, Richard Hamilton, Eduardo Paolozzi and the Memphis designers.

From St. Martins To RCA.

——**So you chose to attend Royal College of Art after graduating from St. Martins?**

At the RCA, I focused on integrating typography with image and not having the two as separate elements. When I was graduating the college said to me, "it might be difficult to find work with your design approach". But immediately I was offered a job by a design company called Lamb and Shirley in 1988 to design the front cover and the intro pages of 'Next Directory' magazine, with a print run of 3 million. I worked on a diverse set of projects when I was there, it was a really great experience and a good training ground.

——**It is quite surprising to know that, your first job as a graphic designer was for traditional print based work.**

It's more normal now to leave college and set up your own studio straight away, but back then it was still rare. I think I was very lucky along the way. I decided to leave Lamb and Shirley and moved to Italy. I worked under the product design guru Michele De Lucchi. I was commissioned by Alessandro Mendini to design a collectors Swatch watch 'Scribble'. On returning, I set up a studio with another designer Jane Chipchase which went well for a while but it was right in the middle of the last recession and after a while we went our separate ways, but I was determined to continue and set up Studio Myerscough in 1993 by myself.

The Influence Of Pop Art.

——**Looking back at your career, what influenced you the most?**

The other day, I did a lecture and the illustrator/educator Lawrence Zeegan attended, and he commented, "your work feels very Pop Art based". I'd never thought about such a direct link before, so when I went back home and looked at all the work hanging on my walls by artists like Andy Warhol, Bridget Riley, Banksy, Jamie Reid, Milton Glazer and Pure Evil, and I thought about what I liked as a student and realized my taste has not changed and his observations were exactly right. Because when I look at those works, I love the instant energy of them, and realized that I don't like work that is laboured over. I think about ideas for a long time, but when the time is right I work extremely fast. That's the way I have always worked.

A Unique Working Process.

——**What process do you work on each project?**

Firstly, a very important element is to have in-depth meetings with your clients or people involved. If you only get a written brief, your understanding of the project is limited, but if you meet directly you can ask a very simple question and it may give you the answer. I like to think things through before I commit to an idea, so the process of meeting in person is very important. After some serious thought on the project, I will research and stimulate my mind with the information. Then various ideas start to emerge. This could be a sketch, a physical model or in different forms, and I'll pin everything up on the walls around my table they become my sketchbook and then further develop these ideas. I have much more confidence in an idea when I have had it surrounding me for a while, when I can really think it through. When I know an idea is right and I present it, I think the people involved can tell and then they trust me to make it happen, trust is one of the most important things.

Place Making.

——**When look objectively, what do you think is distinctive about your work?**

These days, I don't really think of my self as a pure graphic designer. I think there are much better graphic designers around than me. For example, I could be working on an interior of a building, but if I want to design the furniture for that, I won't hesitate to do it. Thinking about space and how people respond to that environment. That's the attitude I always have when I work on a project. The other day, an architect told me that what I do is 'place making', and I think that is a pretty good description. I know this project is about graphic design, so I hope I don't rock the boat (laughs).

STUDIO 8

スタジオ・エイト

ぐるりと外側にデスクが並び、中央には丸いテーブル。壁にはたくさんの書籍と、ポスターやアートが飾られている。ものが多いのに、雑然とした印象を感じないのは、センスの賜物だろうか。物静かなMatt Willeyと明るく親切なZoë Batherが設立したStudio 8。そのスタジオは、気取らない温かさに満ちている。帰り際、飾ってあった彼らのポスターを「かっこいいね」と言うと、お土産に持たせてくれたのだった。

There is a round table in the middle and desks lined all around the outside. The walls are full of posters and art. There are many things, but the reason it doesn't look cluttered is probably due to their sensibilities. Studio 8 was set up by courteous and quiet Matt Willey, and cheerful and kind natured Zoë Bather. The studio is full with warmth and unpretentiousness. On our way out, we complemented a poster they had hung on the wall, and kindly presented it to us as a gift.

2005年、Matt Willey と Zoë Bather により設立。書籍、エキシビション、ウェブサイト、ブランドアイデンティティなど、幅広い分野で活躍している。D&AD、Magnum Photos、Sony、Central School of Speech & Drama など国内外にクライアントに持つほか、雑誌『ELEPHANT Magazine』のアートディレクションも手掛けている。

Founded by Matt Willey and Zoë Bather in 2005. They produce diverse range of work in publishing, exhibitions, websites and brand identities. Working with clients both in the UK and oversee such as D&AD, Magnum Photos, Sony and Central School of Speech & Drama, they also work in art direction for 'ELEPHANT Magazine'.

(Left) Zoë Bather / (Right) Matt Willey

有名スタジオの元同僚コンビ、MattとZoëが独立して設立したStudio 8。きっかけは「たまたま空き部屋が出たからで、特にプランがあったわけじゃない。自分たちはもともと一緒に仕事をしていたからお互いをよく知っていたし、楽しくやっていけると思ったのさ」と、Matt。スタジオ名は、そのオフィスが8号室だったことに由来する。設立当初は雑誌や書籍といったエディトリアルの仕事がメインだったが、近年はブランディングの領域まで幅を広げている。「ちょうどセントラル・スクール・オブ・スピーチ&ドラマのリブランディングの仕事を終えたばかり。うちのクライアントにはギャラリー、フォトグラファー、サーカス学校といったカルチャー系が多く、刺激を受けているわ。小さくても面白そうな仕事をやりたいから、スタッフ数を増やさず小規模のままやっていきたい」(Zoë)。現在のスタッフは4名。インディペンデントならではのユニークな仕事ぶりに、今後も要注目だ。

Ex-colleagues of a famous studio, Studio 8 was set up by the duo of Zoë and Matt. Matt explains the beginnings of their studio, "there just happened to be a spare room, and it wasn't really planned. We worked together before so we knew each other well, and thought we'd have some fun". The name came from that studio, which was room number 8. At the start, their mainly worked on editorials for magazines and books, but recently expanded to include branding. Zoë says, "We've just finished working on the re-branding of the Central School of Speech and Drama. Our clients include many in the cultural field, like galleries, circus schools and photographers, and we are very much influenced by them. Rather than taking on more staff, I'd like stay small so that we can continue working on smaller interesting projects". They added two members of staff currently consist of 4 people. Keep an eye out in future for their unique work typical of their independence.

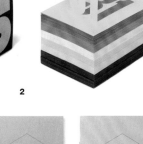

1. 'D&AD Awards Gala 2008' Print / Booklet / D&AD

2. Fedrigoni 2010 Calendar / A Post-It Style Calendar /
Fedrigoni (www.fedrigoni.co.uk) / 2009

3. Size Format Stock / Booklet / Fenner Paper (ww

2

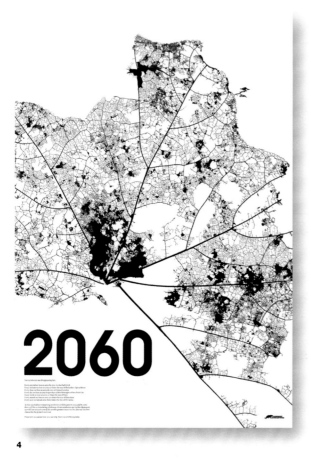

3

1

4

5

6

While chasing after 'for sale' signs, customising his discwheels and nursing his bruises, Andrew Todd gives us an insider view into a sport (and a culture) in the process of being invented, or re-invented

BIKE POLO

Words and photographs by Andrew Todd

7

8

9

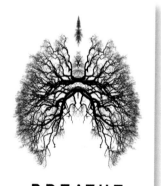

BREATHE

11

CENTRAL

12

dealerward

10

BLAZINGWORD

BLAZINGWORD

BLAZINGWORD

13

LONDON

N°.2 PARIS

14

8, 9. FUTU / Magazine /
Publishing and Design Group Ltd / 2008
10. Dealerward / Identity /
Dealerward Ltd (www.dealerward.com) / 2009
11. BREATHE / Poster / RAN (www.ran.org) /
PH_Giles Revell / 2007
12. Central School of Speech & Drama / Launch Invitations
13. Blazingword / Identity
14. NB Pulse / Travel Guides / Nota Bene Travel / 2007

TAPPIN GOFTON

タッピン・ゴフトン

たくさんのスタッフが働く大企業然としたスタジオ。手掛けてきた作品の規模から、僕たちはそんなイメージを抱いてTappin Goftonの元を訪れた。しかしそこは想像に反して、アンビエントな電子音楽が流れる、作業机と打ち合わせテーブル、本棚だけのミニマルな空間。僕たちの質問に丁寧に回答する2人の姿は、作り上げてきたデザインに対する自信と、何よりデザインへのストイックな姿勢を強く感じさせた。

A large company studio, with a lot of staff. From the scale of their work, that was the impression we had before visiting Tappin Gofton. However to the contrary, it was a minimal space, ambient electronica playing in the background, with a desk, table and bookshelves. In the manner the duo answered our questions so politely, we could sense their confidence towards, and an overall strong stoic attitude, to their design.

2004年、Mark TappinとSimon Goftonにより設立。Coldplay、The Chemical Brothers、Travis、Young Knivesなどの音楽プロジェクトのほか、ファッション、アート、書籍、ウェブサイトなど、幅広い分野でアートディレクション、デザインを手掛けている。

Founded by Mark Tappin and Simon Gofton, Tappin Gofton have worked on music projects with Coldplay, The Chemical Brothers, Travis and Young Knives, as well as designing and art directing in diverse areas such as fashion, art, publishing and websites.

(Left) Mark Tappin / (Right) Simon Gofton

1 / 2 / 3

1, 2, 3. Coldplay / X&Y / Album Campaign / Parlophone
4, 5. Coldplay / Viva La Vida / Album Campaign / Parlophone

1 / 2 / 3

5

1, 2, 3. Young Knives / Voices of Animals and Men /
Album & Identity / Transgressive
4. Rumble Stripes / Identity / Island Records
5. The Feeling / Promo Singles / Island Records
6, 7, 8. Morning Runner / Wilderness Is Paradise Now
/ Album & Identity / Parlophone

6 / 7 / 8

9

9. LeBron Soldier III / Poster Campaign / Nike
10. We Folk / Identity & Website
11. Lalula / Supa Bajo / Single / Bacardi / Elixir Recording
12. Air Traffic / Fractured Life / Album & Singles /
Album & Singles / EMI

WE FOLK

10

11

12

13

15

14

16

13. Travis / The Boy With No Name / Album /
Independiente
14. Paul Quinn /
For What I Have Done And For
What I Have Failed To Do / Book
15. Draft Magazine / Process
16. The Departure / Dirty Words /
Album / Parlophone

1 / 2 / 3

4

1, 2, 3. The Chemical Brothers / We Are The Night / Album
& Single Campaign / Virgin
4. The Chemical Brothers / Brotherhood / Album / Virgin
5. The Chemical Brothers / Push The Botton / Album / Virgin

5

小さなデザインスタジオ"だから"できること。

──まずは、2人がスタジオを設立した経緯を教えてください。

Mark(以下、M):スタジオを設立したのが2004年。当時は小さいデザインスタジオがたくさんできていた時期で、自分たちでやってみるいい機会だと思ったんだ。僕たちは2人とも、10年くらい前にBlue Sourceというデザインスタジオで働いていて、Simonはその後、Tom Hingston Studioで働いていた。ともに長年の経験があったからこそ、その経験を共有して自分たちでスタジオを切り盛りしていくことができると思ったんだ。

小さい規模が可能にすること

──設立したときに、2人の間で何かルールやポリシーなどを決めたのですか?

M:特にそういうものはなかったけれど、"小さい"ことがそのままこのスタジオの特徴になり、強みになったと思う。すべてのプロジェクトについて、全体をコントロールすることができるからね。1ルームに2〜3台のコンピューターという規模が気に入っているし、今までやってきたように、音楽プロジェクトを続けていきたいと思っている。僕たちにとって、イラストレーターやフォトグラファーなど、さまざまなクリエイターと一緒に仕事をしていくのに適した形だし、音楽だけじゃないほかの分野、例えば出版やウェブ、ファッションなどの仕事にもすぐに対応することができる。

Simon(以下、S):小さい規模だからこそ、クライアントに対して、よりパーソナルなレベルでのサービスが提供できる。何か問題が起こったときも、僕たちなら素早く対応することができるしね。

レコードスリーブとUKグラフィックデザイン

──今のUKには、あなたたちのような小規模なデザインスタジオがたくさんあり、シーンを盛り上げていると思います。UKグラフィックシーンには、どんな特徴があると思いますか?

M:誰がどういう見方をするかによって千差万別な見解があると思うけれど、大枠の話をするなら、昔と比べてデジタルメディアが広く普及して、あらゆることが変化しているよね。

S:大きなスタジオが多い、小さなスタジオが多いといったことに関わらず、UKグラフィックシーンは今も昔も非常にクリエイティヴな場所だと思う。"小さい"スタジオであることが僕たちに合っているし、現時点では、それは利点にこそなれ足かせにはならないんだ。

M:大学でグラフィックデザインを勉強している頃、グラフィックデザイナーに一番人気のあったフィールドがスリーブデザインだった。今でもたくさんの若いデザイナーがそのフィールドで活躍している。新しいデザインスタジオを探そうと思ったら、僕たちはデザイン雑誌を読む代わりに、たくさんのレコードスリーブを手に取るんだ。文化レベルでの音楽とのつながりは、UKグラフィックデザインシーンの大きな特徴だよね。

S:一方で、グラフィックデザインシーンだけに注目するよりも、建築や映画、音楽、自然など物事に対して幅広い視点を持っている方が、はるかに面白いことだとも思う。グラフィックシーンの外にあるフィールドが、時にはグラフィックデザインそのものよりも、多くのインスピレーションを僕たちに与えてくれるから。

アートディレクションの過程

──Tappin Goftonは、たくさんの音楽プロジェクトを手掛けていますが、具体的にどういったプロセスで制作が進んでいくのですか?

M:いつも同じなわけではないけれど、たいていの場合、まず最初にミュージシャンとの打ち合わせの場を設け、ディテールを話し合うところから始めている。

S:プロジェクトがスタートすると、全体を包括するアイデアを2人で練っていくんだ。そして、タイポグラフィーやイメージメイキング、イラストレーション、写真など、プロジェクト全体を見通し、必要な要素を話し合う。デザインの土台が固まると、僕たちのうちのどちらかがそのプロジェクトを完成まで導いていく。

小さいスタジオが成した巨大な仕事

──Tappin Goftonと言えば、Coldplay『X&Y』のアートディレクションが印象的です。2人にとって『X&Y』は、どういった位置づけのプロジェクトですか?

S:『X&Y』は、スタジオを設立した初年の仕事で、僕たちにとってもキーになったプロジェクト。今のスタジオよりももっと小さい地下のスペースで、インターナショナルな仕事ができた。長かったけど、すごく楽しい仕事だったよ。

M:プロジェクトは、やはりColdplayのメンバーと会うことから始まった。最初のミーティングでは、具体的にデザインについて話したわけではなく、彼らのアルバムから2〜3曲聴きながら、雑談をした程度。まだ楽曲を制作中だった彼らは、今は制作のどんな段階で、アルバムが何を目指しているのかを話してくれた。その後、僕たちはデザインに関するたくさんのコンセプト案を考え、アイデアソースを集めた。Coldplayからもいくつかアイデアの提案があり、それと僕たちのアイデアをミックスして、ひとつのコンセプトが決まったんだ。このプロセスに、5〜6ヵ月くらいの時間を要して、ようやく最終型のデザインに辿りついた。インターナショナルなプロジェクトだったから、たくさんのメディアに僕たちのアートワークが使われたし、ライブやマーチャンダイズ、ウェブサイトなどのスタイルも、それを元に展開していったんだ。

キャリアや設備よりも大切なもの

──全世界で展開されたプロジェクトのアートディレクションを、たった2人で手掛けたんですね。
M:このスタジオの半分しかないフロアには、2〜3台のコンピューターと電話とインターネットアクセスだけ。そんな小さな規模で、世界的なプロジェクトを成功させることができたんだ。キャリアがなくても十分な設備が整ってなくても、アイデアと情熱さえ持っていれば、たくさんのことが可能になる。僕たちはそれを証明したのさ。

What A Design Studio Is Capable Because It Is "Small".

——**Firstly, how did the two of you start your studio?**

Mark (M): The studio was set up in 2004. At this time, there were many smaller design studios opening up. We both worked for a studio called Blue Source about 10 years ago, and Simon then left to work for Tom Hingston Studio. So we both had enough experience and decided to use that to set something up our selves.

Possibilities With In A Small Scale Makes Possible.

——**When you set up, did you make any rules or policies between each other?**

M: Not anything in particular, but I think keeping it "small" became part our studio's character and strength. In that way, we can control the whole process of every project. I like the fact that we have one room with two or three computers, and we're keen to continue our music projects. Our size suits working with different creative people like illustrators and photographers, and enables us not to just work with the music industry but in other areas like publishing, web or fashion.

Simon (S): Being a small studio, we can give clients a more personal level of service. Even if there are any problems, we are able to react quickly to resolve any issues.

Record Sleeves And UK Graphic Design.

——**Currently in the UK, I think there are many smaller scale design studios like your selves lifting the scene. What kind of characteristics do you think the UK graphic scene has?**

M: I think depending on how you look at it you can have many different points of view, but if your talking about an overview, compared to the past digital media is more prevalent now and so everything is shifting.

S: Regardless of the size, the UK graphic design scene is, and always has been, an incredibly creative one. Being a 'small' studio suits us and at this point in time, it's an advantage not a hindrance.

M: When I was studying graphic design at college, the most popular field amongst graphic designers was record sleeve design. Even now, many young designers are active in that field. If we were looking for a new design studio, we wouldn't look through design magazines, but look through record sleeves. I think the link with music at a cultural level is a unique part of the UK graphic design scene.

S: I think it's far more interesting to not just focus on a the graphic design scene, but to look at what's happening in the world of architecture, art, film or music and nurture a broader perspective on things. The fields outside of the graphic design scene are often more of an inspiration to us than graphic design.

The Process Of Art Direction.

——**Tappin Gofton work on many music projects, but can you tell us about the process in which your work develops?**

M: It's not always the same, but firstly we set up a meeting with the musicians and begin to discuss the details.

S: When a project starts, the two of us will work together on developing ideas. We'll discuss typography, image making, illustration, photography, basically whatever the overall project requirements are. Once the project has been established one of us will see the project through to completion.

A Large Project Undertaken By A Small Studio.

——**When you think of Tappin Gofton, the art direction of Coldplay's 'X&Y' springs to mind. How important was this project to the both of you?**

S: We started working on 'X&Y' in the first year we began our studio, and it was a key project for us. We worked on this international project in a basement studio smaller that our current one. It was long, but a really enjoyable project.

M: As always, we began the project by meeting the members of Coldplay. There, we didn't talk specifically about the design but just hang out with the band, listening to 2 or 3 songs. As they were still in the process of making the record, they talked about where they were and the direction they were going. After that, we thought about different concepts and gathered many idea sources. Coldplay had some ideas to share, so we mixed them with ours, and came up with the concept. This process took 5 to 6 months before we reached the final stage. It was an international project so our art work was used in different ways, and live shows, merchandise and the website came out of that.

Something More Important Than Career Or Facilities.

——So you worked on the art direction of a project that expanded worldwide, with just two people.

M: In the space of half this studio, we just had a few computers, a phone, and Internet connection. We were able to make a success of a worldwide project, even from this small size. Even if you don't have a huge career and have brilliant facilities, if you have a good idea and passion, you can do a lot. We proved that's possible.

TOM HINGSTON STUDIO

トム・ヒングストン・スタジオ

イーストロンドンばかりを動き回っていた僕たちは、取材5日目にして初めてロンドンの中心（かつ観光拠点としても名高い）、ピカデリー・サーカス駅を訪れた。歴史を感じさせる美しい建築が並ぶリージェント・ストリートのすぐ裏手に、Tom Hingston Studioは位置している。多忙にも関わらず、快く応じてくれたインタビュー。彼は、懐かしい記憶を辿るように、ゆっくりと20年前の出来事を語り始めた。

We had spent a great deal of time walking around east London, but on our 5th day headed into the center for Piccadilly Circus station (the famous tourist destination). Tom Hingston's studio is situated just behind Regent Street and all its beautiful architecture steeped in history. He kindly complied with our interview, regardless of his busy day. Then began speaking about his 20 year career as though he was tracing back fond memories.

1990年代初期、イーストロンドンのクラブBlue Noteのヴィジュアル制作を担当した後、1997年にスタジオ設立。Massive Attack、Robbie Williams、The Rolling Stonesなどの音楽プロジェクトのほか、ファッション、広告、ブランディングなど、その活動は幅広い。Alexander McQueen、BBC、Christian Dior、Nikeなどのクライアントを持つ。

After contributing to the visual imaging of east London club Blue Note, in the early 1990's, he founded his studio in 1997. His music projects include Massive Attack, Robbie Williams and The Rolling Stones, and he also works across a wide range of fields spanning fashion advertising and banding. His other clients include Alexander McQueen, BBC, Christian Dior and Nike.

Tom Hingston

1

2

1. Massive Attack / Heligoland /
Cover Art_Robert Del Naja
2. Massive Attack / Collected /
Cover PH_Nick Knight, Book PH_David Hughes
3. Massive Attack / 100th Window /
PH_Nick Knight
4. Massive Attack / Mezzanine /
PH_Nick Knight

3 / 4

183

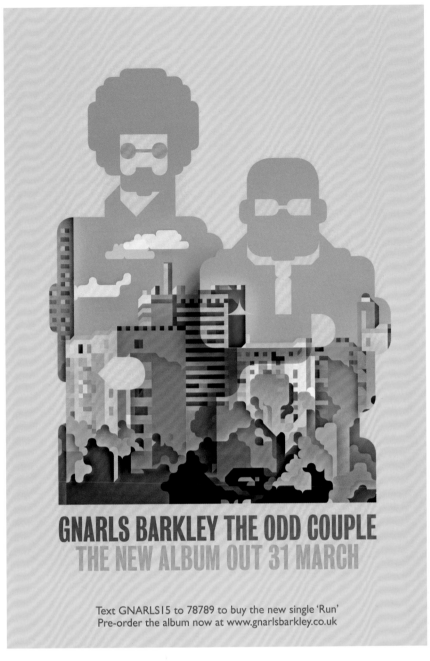

5. Gnarls Barkley / The Odd Couple / IL_Siggi Eggertsson
6. Gnarls Barkley / Crazy / IL_Kam Tang
7. Gnarls Barkley / St. Elsewhere / IL_Kam Tang
8. Gnarls Barkley / Smiley Faces / IL_Kam Tang

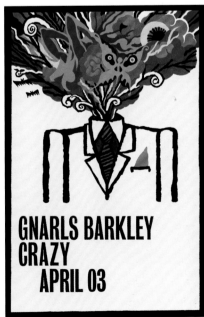

5 / 6 / 7 / 8

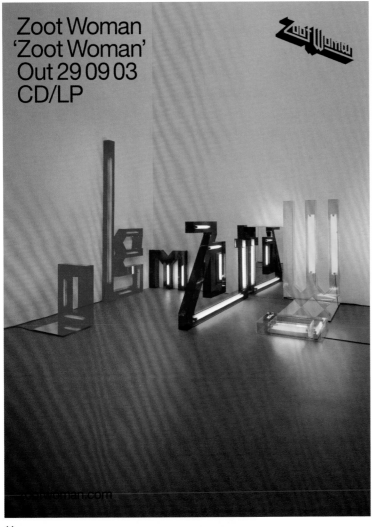

Zoot Woman
'Zoot Woman'
Out 29 09 03
CD/LP

11

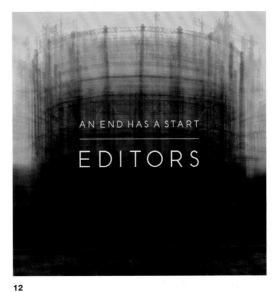

AN END HAS A START

EDITORS

12

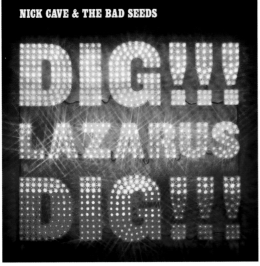

NICK CAVE & THE BAD SEEDS

DIG!!!
LAZARUS
DIG!!!

13

GRACE JONES   HURRICANE

14

9. Prét a Porter Paris AW 2010 /
PH_Warren du Preez and Nick Thornton Jones
10. Prét a Porter Paris AW 2009 / PH_Luis Sanchis
11. Zoot Woman / Zoot Woman /
PH_Anuschka Blommers and Niels Schumm
12. Nick Cave & The Bad Seeds / Dig Lazarus Dig!!! /
Sculpture_Tim Noble and Sue Webster,
PH_David Hughes
13. Editors / An End Has A Start / IL_Idris Khan
14. Grace Jones / Hurricane / PH_Jonathan De Villiers

BAIBAKOV

1

FLUTTER & WOW

2

3

COPENHAGEN

7

B

8

9

RADIAL

13

CP

14

15

TBC

19

TBC

20

TBC

21

25

26

4

5

6

10

11

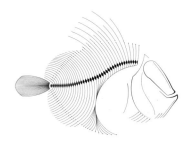

12

16

17

18

22

23

24

音楽とグラフィックデザインの、良好な関係。

――Tom Hingstonという名前を初めて世に知らしめたのは、イーストロンドンのホクストン・スクエアにあった伝説的なクラブ、ブルーノートの仕事だったと記憶しています。

当時、僕はNeville Brodyのスタジオに勤めていて、彼のところにいた3年半の間、個人的にもたくさんのデザインを手掛けていたんだ。その中心はブルーノートの仕事で、あの頃は、毎晩のようにイベントのフライヤーやポスター、ロゴなんかをデザインしていたね。次第にクラブの人気が高まると、それにともなってデザインの仕事も増えていった。最初は週に3〜4枚ほどデザインしていたフライヤーが、10枚、15枚になった。その頃は実質的に2つの仕事を持っているようなもので、もうこれ以上この状態を続けていくことは難しいと感じ、独立を決めたんだ。ちょうど12年前のことだね。

スタジオの始まり

――スタジオ設立当初は、やはりブルーノートの仕事がほとんどだったのですか？

スタジオを始めたとき、クライアントはごくわずかで、ブルーノートと、今はもうない3つのインディペンデントなレコードレーベルくらいだった。すごく小規模なところからのスタートだったよ。僕が仕事をしていたのは、DJやミュージシャン、またはプロモーターなど、クラブと何かしらのつながりがある人たちだった。彼らとのコラボレーションは本当にエキサイティングで、そのとき起こっていた生の喧噪を味わえたんだ。

――当時はどこにスタジオを構えていたのですか？

最初からこの場所だよ。当時、このビルの上の階には『Dorado』というレコードレーベルがあったんだ。（インタビューを行った）この部屋はそのレーベルのストアで、たくさんのレコードが並んでいた。僕はここに積んであった段ボール箱を部屋の隅にまとめて、自分のデスクを置いたのさ。最初の1年半は、週25ポンドで間借りしたこのスペースのデスクと僕が、スタジオのすべてだった。そこから少しずつ成長していったんだ。

音楽からキャリアを始める理由

――あなたをはじめUKの著名グラフィックデザイナーには、音楽の仕事からキャリアをスタートさせた人がたくさんいます。その理由は何だと思いますか？

音楽は常に文化的に重要な位置を担っていて、実験的なヴィジュアルを試す機会にめぐまれている分野。だから歴史的にも、たくさんのデザイナーがそこからキャリアをスタートさせてきたんだと思う。絵を描くための真っ白なキャンバスを与えられるようなものだからね。残念なことに、今はそういう傾向が影を潜めていて、クリエイティヴに重きを置くよりも販売戦略に基づいた決定がなされる場合が多くなってしまった。

過去20年間でデザインシーンに起こった変化

――スタジオを設立した20年前と比べて、今のUKグラフィックデザインシーンはどう変わったと思いますか？

一番大きな変化は、小規模でインディペンデントなスタジオがすごく増えたことだね。6〜7年前、たくさんのデザイナーが大規模なデザインスタジオを辞めて、自分たちのスタジオを設立した。BibliothèqueのJonとMasonがFarrow DesignとNorthを辞め、Universal EverythingのMatt PykeがThe Designers Republicから独立したようにね。今、UKには、彼らのような小さいスタジオがたくさんあり、みんな素晴らしい仕事をしている。デジタルテクノロジーの発達がその大きな理由だろうね。大掛かりな設備がなくても、動画や印刷物など、たくさんの異なるメディアを横断してデザインすることがすごく簡単になったから。

――それはデザイナー側の変化なのか、仕事を発注するクライアント側の変化なのか、どちらの影響が大きいのでしょうか？

UKグラフィックデザインシーンを見渡したとき、今はシーンそのものが再構築されている時期のように思える。クライアントは大きなデザインスタジオや広告代理店と仕事をする必要がないことを理解し始めた。彼らの仕事のやり方は、常に大荷物を抱えているようなもので、その大仰さは古くさくなった。今や5〜6人の規模のスタジオでも才能のあるデザイナーと仕事をすることができるし、小規模であればクライアントとよりパーソナルな関係を築くこともできる。現に、小さなエージェンシーが大きなエージェンシーから仕事を勝ち取っているし、そういったことは数年前では起こりえなかった。僕たちにとっても、こういう風潮はエキサイティングな可能性を与えてくれている。

仕事を厳選していくこと

――仕事をするうえで、今、最も興味のあるフィールドは何でしょう。

僕たちのクライアントワークは、音楽、映像、ブランディング、広告など、極めて幅広く展開していて、異なるフィールドを横断しながら仕事をしている。僕自身

もその多様なクリエイティヴを楽しんでいるし、すごく健全なことだと思う。ここ数年は映像と広告の仕事が増えてきていて、この2つはこれから続けたいし開拓していきたい分野だ。もちろん音楽のプロジェクトも相変わらず楽しんでやっているよ。主に仕事をしているのは、Massive AttackやGnarls Barkley、Nick Caveなど、長年の信頼関係があるミュージシャンだけれど、去年発売されたGrace Jonesのアルバムのような新規のプロジェクトも進めている。ただやはり音楽という分野に限定すれば、手掛けるプロジェクトはすごく厳選されたものだね。

プリントメディアから映像メディアへ

──今後、どのようなプロジェクトを手掛けていきたいと思っていますか?

今、ちょうどAnton Corbijnの新作映画『The American』のタイトルデザインを手掛けているんだけれど、今後、こういう映像メディアの仕事をもっと増やしていきたいと思っている。10年前は、広告と言えば街頭ビルボードや雑誌が主流だったけれど、今は映像をベースにしたメディアが多くなった。世界中の大都市で、かつてポスターが貼られていた場所には、映像が流れるモニターが設置されている。すべてがそういう方向にシフトしているし、それが僕たちが映像をベースにしたプロジェクトに夢中になる理由なんだ。

The Positive Relationship Between Music And Graphic Design.

——As I recall, the name Tom Hingston began to appear frequently after you started doing work for the Blue Note club in Hoxton Square east London.

At the time I was working at Neville Brody's studio, and during those three and a half years, I also began to work on a lot of self-initiated projects. The main bulk of those were for the Blue Note club, and I would spend almost every night designing flyers, posters and logos for club nights. As the club grew in reputation, my workload increased. What was initially 3 or 4 flyers a week, gradually became 10 or 15. Essentially I had two jobs and it was becoming increasingly difficult to juggle both, so I made the decision to leave Neville's and set up on my own. It's exactly 12 years ago now.

The Beginnings Of The Studio.

——When you initially set up your own studio, were you mainly working for Blue Note?

When I started out, I only had a handful of clients, Blue Note and three other independent record labels. Really very small beginnings. That circle of people were all individuals that were somehow connected through the club - either DJs, musicians or promoters. It was an exciting time as there was a real buzz and collaborative spirit around everything we did together.

——Where was your studio located at the time?

It was here from the beginning. At the time, there was a record label on the floor above mine called 'Dorado'. This room (where the interview is held) was their store room, packed full of records. I moved the boxes to one corner and placed my desk in the other. For the first year and a half I paid £25 a week for the space and the studio was just the desk and myself, and it slowly grew from there.

The Reason For Starting One's Career Through Music.

——Many established designers, including you, seem to have started their career through work with music. Why do you think that is?

Music obviously carries huge cultural significance and in doing so has always been a platform which has embraced visual experimentation. So I think that's why historically a lot of young designers have started their careers in this area - engaging with the blank canvas so to speak. Unfortunately that latitude for experimentation is much less so nowadays... Decisions tend to be based on marketing strategies rather than creative ideas.

The Change In The Design Scene In The Past 20 Years.

——How has the UK graphic design scene changed since you set up your studio 20 years ago?

I think the biggest change has been in the increase in smaller, independent studios. There was a period 6 or 7 years ago where many designers broke away from bigger design companies to establish their own, people like Jon and Mason of Bibliothèque leaving Farrow Design and North or Matt Pyke of Universal Everything leaving The Designers Republic. There are a lot of small studios producing brilliant work in the UK at the moment. Largely due to the evolution of technology it's much easier for a smaller set up to work across very diverse media, such as motion, sound and print.

——Is that due to the change with the designers or the change in clients who request work? Whose influence do you think is greater?

When I look at the design scene in the UK, I feel like we're in a period of real transition. Clients are beginning to understand that they don't necessarily need to work with the big design studios or ad agencies any longer. They bring too much baggage and their whole business model is outdated. You can work with a highly talented and specialized team of 5 or 6 individuals who really know their craft and can nurture a more personal relationship with a client. This is evident in us seeing smaller boutique agencies winning big accounts from larger agencies, something which simply wouldn't have happened several years ago. Personally I think that holds really exciting potential.

Stringent Selection Of Work.

——**What field are you most interested to work in?**

Our client base is extremely diverse and we work across many different fields including music, moving image, branding and advertising. I really enjoy that diversity - creatively, it's very healthy and I'd like it to remain that way. In recent years we've been producing a lot more moving image and advertising work - those are certainly two areas I'd like to continue to explore further. On the music side of things we still enjoy working with certain artists, particularly people we have a long standing relationship with, such as Massive Attack, Gnarls Barkley or Nick Cave. And then of course there are also new projects that come along which are really interesting - like the Grace Jones album that we designed last year for instance. On the whole though, we tend to be very selective about the music projects we take on these days.

From Print Media To Motion Media.

——**In the future what kind of project are you looking forward to take on?**

We're currently designing the titles for Anton Corbijn's new film 'The American' - I really enjoy those projects and it's definitely something we'd like to do more of. 10 years ago, traditional advertising media meant big billboards and magazines but now motion based media is on the rise – there's a noticeable shift occurring. Walking around any major city you'll notice that many of the poster sites that once featured print media have now been swapped for screens. Everything seems to be gravitating in that direction, which is one of the reasons why we're excited about taking on more moving image based projects.

TOMATO

トマト

現在10人のクリエイターを擁するTomato。John Warwickerがオーストラリアのメルボルンに在住しているように、国外を拠点に活動するメンバーも多い。今回、イーストロンドンのスタジオで待っていてくれたのは、創立メンバーのひとりSimon Taylor。穏やかな語り口の彼だが、インタビューの最後、制作中の作品について楽しそうに話す姿は、無邪気という表現が一番ふさわしいように思えた。

Tomato currently consist of 10 creators. Many of their members are based oversees, as is John Warwicker who resides in Australia. One of the founding members, Simon Taylor awaited us in their east London studio. He spoke in a very calm manner, but in fact, after seeing the way he joyfully explained his current projects towards the end of the interview, innocent may be the description that suits him most.

多分野のクリエイターが集まったクリエイティヴ集団として、1991年に設立。映画『Trainspotting』のオープニングムービーやSony、NikeのTVCFなどの映像作品のほか、Tomato内のユニットUnderworldによる音楽からのアプローチなど、その表現方法は多彩。グラフィックデザイン、ウェブサイト、インテリア、建築など多方面で活躍する。

Founded in 1991 as a collective of artist from different backgrounds. Their creative output is varied, from video work for Sony and Nike's TVCF, and the opening sequence of the film 'Trainspotting', to their music from Tomato's own musical unit Underworld. They are active in areas of graphic design, websites, interiors, and architecture.

Simon Taylor

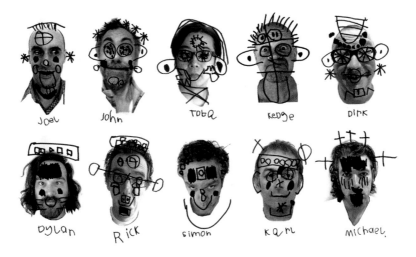

1

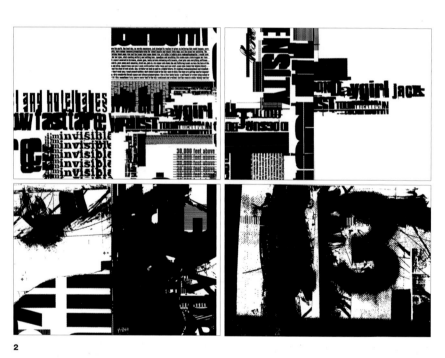

2

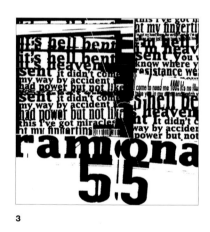

3

1. Trainspotting / Film Title Sequence / 1996
2. Mmm... Skyscraper I Love You / Book / 1994
3. Ramona 55 / Record Sleeve / 1994
4. Beaucoup Fish / CD Packaging / 1999

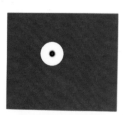

4

5. Speednick / Tune up / Beautiful Poetry Cheap
Sentiment / Merchandise / 1993
6. Cowgirl / Video Stills / 1994

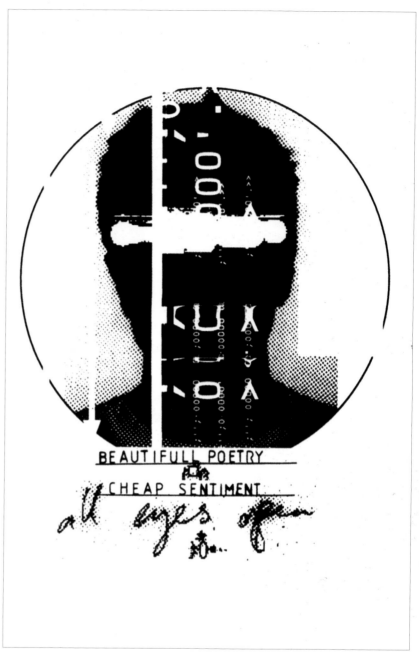

5

5

1

2

3

1, 2, 3. Tokyo < = > London / Exhibition / Japan 1997
4. Un Movil en Patera / Exhibition / Spain 2003
5. TV Asahi / Branding / 2002
6. Nostalgia / Exhibition / Italy 2004

4

6

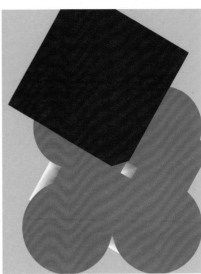

7. Gasbook / Book Cover / 2002
8, 9. Sony PS2 / Advertising Campaign / 2003
10. Sony C.I / Branding / 2001

7

8

You know me. I am sound. I am thought. I am form. I am light. Just ju-ju.

9

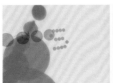

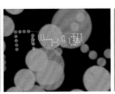

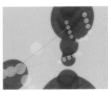

10

1. Floating World / Book / 2009
2. G8 / Logo / 2008
3. There & Back / Again / Exhibition with Sir Peter Blake / South Korea 2009
4. Art & Australia / Logo / 2009

5. Nouvelle Vague 3 / CD Packaging / 2009
6. Nouvelle Vague 3 / Numericals / 2009

5

6

多彩な個性が押し広げる、デザインのフィールド。

——TomatoとUnderworldが強く結びついているように、UKグラフィックシーンは音楽とのつながりが、とりわけ強いように感じます。あなたから見た、UKグラフィックシーンの特徴とは何ですか?

UKグラフィックデザインシーンにとって音楽はなくてはならないものだと思う。1960年代以降、ロンドンのミュージックシーンはすごく活発で、たくさんの才能を世に送り出してきた。例えばパリやマドリッドなど、ほかのどの都市を見渡しても、ロンドンほど強くて濃密なミュージックシーンはない。過去数十年、UKグラフィックデザインシーンは音楽とともに発展してきたと言えるだろうね。

デジタルテクノロジーがもたらしたもの

——では、現在の状況をどう見ていますか?

デジタルテクノロジーの発達で、すべてに変化がもたらされたよね。グラフィックデザイン以外にも映像、音楽、写真など、デジタルテクノロジーを介せば、さまざまなメディアがコミュニケーションの媒体になることができる。また、ここ十数年の間に、モバイルコミュニケーションとウェブコミュニケーションはなくてはならないものになった。その変化は、個人や小さいグループなどの創作活動を後押ししていると思う。作品を制作することも発表することも、昔と比べてすごく簡単になったし、実際、至るところにクリエイターが存在している。

——特に、グラフィックデザインシーンについてはどうでしょう。

僕が重要視しているのは、デジタルツールがもたらした"アクセスの容易さ"なんだ。つまり、グラフィックデザイナー側にとっては多くの作品を簡単に発表できるようになり、見る側にとってはいつでもどこからでも簡単にデザイナーの作品を見ることができるようになった。こういう気軽さが年々増してきているのは、すごく注目すべきことだと思う。

Tomatoがスタートした理由

——ところで、Tomatoを始めたきっかけは何だったのでしょうか?

グラフィックデザイナーや3Dデザイナー、ミュージシャン、ライターなど、それぞれ違った要素を持ったクリエイティヴな職業の人たちが集まり、グループを結成したんだ。たぶんその頃、仕事として作品を作ることに、みんな不満を持っていたんだと思う。Tomatoはクリエイティヴな集団であり、会社ではなかった。集団に多様性を持たせたのは、お互いが異なるメッセージを発信しながら、異なる仕事のやり方を知ることで、各個人の仕事が持っている限界を押し広げたかったから。それと、経済的な意味で助け合うことができたのも大きな利点だった。スタジオ維持費や設備費などの支払いに頭を悩ませることなく、それぞれが制作に集中できたからね。

——Tomatoがスタートしたとき、グループとしてのルールや理念などはあったのでしょうか?

最初はなかったよ。ただ、すでに見たことのあるもの、知っているものを作るのだけは絶対にやめて、常に新しいものを生み出そうという気持ちをみんなが持っていたと思う。そして数年後、この考え方に基づいた制作のプロセスが、僕たちのフィロソフィーになった。

スタジオとしての強み、面白み

——過去に影響を受けたものや人はありますか?

映画監督、ペインター、詩人、作家、ミュージシャン、彫刻家、建築家、ファッションデザイナーなど、無数にありすぎて特定の名前を挙げることができないよ。目を開けている間ずっと、誰かや何かにインスピレーションを受けているわけだから。

——あなたから見たTomatoの特徴、スタジオとしての強みとは何でしょうか?

Tomatoはグラフィックデザインのスタジオでもないし、音楽スタジオでも映画スタジオでもない。言うなれば、それらすべてを統合したクリエイティヴな集合体。人は誰かの作品を見たとき、「これはNeville Brodyのデザイン」「これはJonathan Barnbrookの」「これはTomatoの」というふうに、作品のテイストから作家を予想することが多い。でも僕は、そういう"誰々っぽい"というのが好きじゃないし、きっとほかのメンバーもそうだと思う。なぜなら、そういう"っぽさ"は、自らのクリエイティヴィティに限界を作ってしまうことだし、同時に見てくれる人の想像力にも限界を設けてしまうことだからね。Tomatoの一連の作品を見ると、さまざまなテイストが混在していることがわかる。ハンドペイントのような激情的な作品から、配置する要素が計算されたシャープな作品まで、さまざまなテイストが同時に存在している。

独特の制作スタイル

——Tomatoのポートフォリオを見ると実験的な作品が多く、クライアントから依頼を受けて制作したものと、個人的な欲求で制作したものの境が曖昧なように思えます。

Tomatoは面白いスタジオなんだ。たくさんのパーソナルなプロジェクトと同時に、それ以上の数のクライアントワークが進行していて、この2つの要素が交差し関連している。過去に作ったものに対して、クライアントが自分たちの意向にふさわしい意味を見出したり、制作中の作品が商業的なプロジェクトに膨らんでいったりと、パーソナルワークがクライアントワークにつながっていく。それが僕たちのスタイル。もし、すべてがクライアントワークだったら、常に誰かのために創作することになる。それで彼らの目的を達成することはできるけれど、いったい自分たちのゴールはどこにある？　クライアントワークとパーソナルワークのバランスが大事なんだ。

時間をデザインすること

——今、一番興味のある表現分野は何ですか？

Tomatoのメンバーそれぞれが違う視点を持っていると思うけれど、個人的なことを言えば、"時間をともなうメディア"に興味がある。例えば、ミュージックフィルムやパフォーマンスアートなどには、始まりと終わり、時間の流れが存在するよね。そういうメディアにおいては、視覚的なイメージだけでなく時間の流れもプランニングする必要がある。時間を軸に、音、光、感覚、感情などのすべてが結びついた体験の提供。僕にとって今一番興味があるのは、そういう時間の積み重ねをクリエイトすることなんだ。今もアクターやミュージシャンと一緒に、映像を絡めた劇場パフォーマンスの作品を制作している。大きなプロジェクトではないけれど、すごく実験的で面白い作品に仕上がると思うよ。

Field Of Design, Where Diverse Talents Flourish.

——**Similar to your strong link with Underworld, there seems to be a strong link between the UK graphic design scene and music. What do you think is characteristic about the UK graphic scene?**

I think music is something essential to the UK graphic scene. After the 1960's, the music scene in London was very active and gave the world many musical talents. For example, if you look at different cities like Paris or Madrid, there is no scene as dense or strong. You could say that the UK graphic design scene has developed together over the course of the last few decades.

Effect Of Technology.

——**How do you see the current situation?**

Technological development has affected everything. Not just graphic design, but through the use of digital technology, such as music and photography, all these types of media become a platform for communication. Again, in the past few decades, mobile and web communication has also become essential. I think these changes are helping to support the work of individuals or smaller groups. Presenting and making work has become a lot easier, and the fact that there are creators everywhere now, is proof.

——**What do you think specifically about the graphic design scene?**

I'm interested in the "easiness of accessibility" the digital tool has brought. Therefore, for graphic designers it means it's easier to present work, and for the viewer it's easy to access the work of designers. This accessibility is increasing every year, and this is something very important.

The Reason Tomato Began.

——**So, what was the reason for starting Tomato?**

We formed a group of people with different influences from various creative backgrounds, such as graphic and 3D designers, musicians and writers. I think we were all dissatisfied with where we were supposed to work in the industry. We were a creative unit, and not a company. The reason for creating this collective was to push each others boundaries a little, by understanding the discipline in varying fields, whilst introducing different messages. Also, another advantage was that we were able to support each other financially. We could all concentrate on our work instead of worrying about studio and maintenance fees.

——**Was there a collective rule or philosophy behind Tomato at the start?**

Immediately no. We rejected anything we knew of, or seen before, and constantly tried to do something different. After a couple of years, this process behind the ideas became our philosophy.

The Strength And Excitement Of The Studio.

——**Is there anything or anyone who influenced you in the past?**

There are film directors, painters, poets, writers, musicians, sculptors, architects and fashion designers. Too many to single one out. I am constantly keeping my eyes open, getting inspiration from someone or something.

——**What do you regard to be the characteristics or strengths of Tomato?**

Tomato isn't a graphic design studio, nor is it a music or film studio. It's a creative bloc integrating everything. People always try to guess who the creator is from the style, "that's Neville Brody's, that's Jonathan Barnbrook's and that's Tomato's," but I don't really like that and I'm sure the others are the same. That's because it's limiting to your own creativity, and at the same time limiting the imagination of the viewer. If you take a look at all our work, you can see the mix of taste. Diverse styles converge, on one hand there's an emotive hand paint-looking pieces, and on the other a clean sharp considered piece.

A Distinct Production Style.

——**When you look at the Tomato portfolio there are many experimental works, and there seems to be a blurring of the lines between commissioned work from clients and personally inspired work.**

Tomato is an interesting studio. There are a lot personal projects going on, but at the same time even more client work, and the two elements are overlap and connect. In previous work, clients would find meaning suited to them, or something your personally working on may develop into commercial work, so personal and client work become connected. That's our style. But if all our work was for clients, you constantly end up working for somebody else. You can satisfy their goals, but where do ours lie? So it is important to have the right balance of client work and personal work.

Designing Time.

——**What media are you interested in the most at the moment?**

Every person has a different point of view in Tomato, but personally I'm interested in 'time-based media'. For example, in music films, or performance art, there is a passing of time. For that type of media, you have to plan the visual aspect as well as the flow of time. It seems to offer you a bond between sound, space, senses and emotions. For me, creating this stack of time is what is interesting the most. At the moment, together with an actor and a musician, I'm planning a theatrical performance piece tied in with visuals. It's not a big project, but I'm sure it's going to be a very experimental and exciting piece.

WOOD McGRATH

ウッド・マックグラス

数人でシェアするスタジオの一角、デスク2つ分のスペースがWood McGrathのアトリエだ。デスクまわりや本棚には、彼らの作品に交じって、デザインのインスピレーションになっているのだろうか、古い書籍や画集もちらほら。ビスケットとコーヒーで僕たちを迎えてくれた物腰柔らかな2人と話していると、作品が持つお洒落で優しい雰囲気にも納得がいく。卓上のチューリップが、とても彼ららしいと感じた。

Placed in the corner of their shared studio, Wood McGrath's atelier consists of two desks. Around the desk and on the walls, old books and catalogues are found placed among their own work, we assume it's their design inspiration. They welcome us with coffee and biscuits, and talking to the soft-natured duo, we understand where the edgy but delicate feel in their work comes from. The tulip on the desk, seemed to exemplify that.

『Dazed & Confused』のアートディレクターを務めたSuzy Woodと、セント・マーチンズで教鞭をとっていたMartin McGrathの2人により、2007年に設立。書籍、アート、カルチャー、パフォーミングアート、ファッションなど、幅広い範囲で活躍中。また、雑誌『Lula』のアートディレクションも務めていた。

Formed in 2007 by former 'Dazed & Confused' art director Suzy Wood, and former St. Martins tutor, Martin McGrath. They work in a diverse range of area such as art, culture, publishing, performing art and fashion. They were also art directors for 'Lula' magazine.

(Left) Suzy Wood / (Right) Martin McGrath

SuzyとMartinが出会ったのは4年前。たまたまジンのプロジェクトで一緒になって以来、あまりに気が合うので自然とチームを組むようになった。「もともと私が借りていたスタジオに、彼が来るようになったのよ。最初はひとつのデスクを共有していたから、ちょっと狭かったわ」とSuzy。スタジオの名前は2人のラストネームをつなげた。どこかファンタジックで可愛らしい彼らの作品のルーツは、古い雑誌や本にあると言う。Martinは「小さい頃から本に夢中で、本のデザインは自分にとって特別だったんだ」、Suzyは「グラフィックデザイナーだった祖父の影響が大きいわ。私が生まれる前に彼は亡くなったけれど、母が作品と美しい万年筆などの仕事道具を取っておいて、私に渡してくれたの」。そんな彼らが2009年、建築デザインスタジオ、アーバン・サロン・アーキテクツのプロジェクトを手掛けた。「エキシビションやショップをデザインする一連のプロジェクトだったんだ」と、生き生きとした表情で語る2人が印象的だった。

Suzy and Martin met 4 years ago. They happened to work on a fanzine project together, and as they got on so well, naturally formed a team. "Originally he would come to the studio I was renting. At first we were sharing one desk between us so it was bit of a squeeze," says Suzy. They came up with the name of the studio by combining their surnames. Their work has something sweet and fantasy-like about them, which they say may have roots in old books and magazines. Martin states, "I've loved books from when I was little, and the design of a book was very important to me," and Suzy recalls, "I was influenced by my grandfather, who was a graphic designer. He died just before I was born, but my mother kept some of his work and equipment - beautiful script pens and type rules, which were passed on to me". In 2009, "we collaborated with Urban Salon Architects on a series of projects designing for exhibitions and retail," they said in their colorful expressions.

Qu'est-ce qu'un miroir?

What is a mirror?

1, 2. Love From… / Booklet /
Wood McGrath Collaboration with Clare Shilland & Beth Fenton / 2009

1

2

3

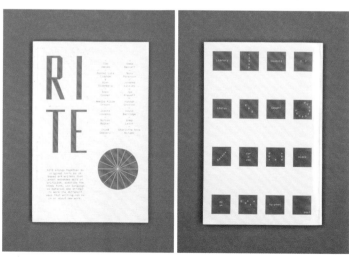

4

5

1. Design Architecture and Cultural Relations Newsletter,
Autumn 2008 / Booklet / British Council / 2008
2. Design Architecture and Cultural Relations Newsletter,
Spring 2008 / Booklet / British Council / 2008
3. International Young Design Entrepreneur of the Year Award /
Poster / British Council / 2007
4. Maharaja, The Splendour of India's Royal Courts / Exhibition /
Victoria & Albert Museum, London / 2009
5. RITE / Book / New Work Net Work, Open Dialogues / 2009

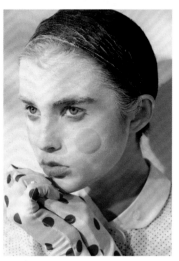

Why Don't
They Let Us
Fall In Love?

LIVE AS YOU DREAM

IN FLIGHTS OF
FANCY & VISIONS
OF BEAUTY

Photography by CATHERINE SERVEL
Beauty by SAM BRYANT

Once Upon a Time

By RACHEL THOMAS

Lula / Magazine / Lula Publishing / 2010

イエス

ショーディッチ・ハイストリート駅から北に少し歩くと、YESがスタジオを構えるヴィクトリア調の建物ロシェルスクールが見えてくる。1895年に建てられ、小学校として使われていた建物は、現在デザインスタジオやギャラリーが入居する、クリエイティヴスペースとして再生している。James Musgraveと雑談していると、別のミーティングから自転車で駆けつけたSimon Earithが、息を切らしながら現れた。

After a short walk from Shoreditch High Street station, we arrive at a Rochelle School, a Victorian era building where YES is situated. Built in 1895, the building was previously used as a primary school, but now reinvented as a creative space housing many studios and a gallery space. As we were early we began by having a chat with senior designer James Musgrave, and a little later YES founder Simon Earith appears, out of breath after a bike ride, returning from a meeting in central London.

Blue Sourceでクリエイティヴディレクターを務めていたSimon Earithによって、2004年に設立。現在はJames Musgrave、James 'Homer' Homer を加えた3人で活動している。音楽プロジェクトのアートディレクションを中心に、ギャラリーやレコードレーベル、写真家、アーティストなど多様なクライアントを持つ。

Established in 2004 by former Blue Source creative director Simon Earith, YES now has three full-time studio members with the addition of James Musgrave and James 'Homer' Homer. The initial focus on work for the music industry has now developed into a diverse mix, working for galleries, photographers, artists and record labels.

(Left) James Musgrave / (Right) Simon Earith

プラスするのではなく、引き算のデザインアプローチで知られるYES。創設者のSimonは「必要な要素が見えるまでそぎ落としていくこと、それが自分たちの手法。そうすることによって、シンプルかつエレガントで、明確なメッセージを持ったデザインができあがる。そのためにはコラボレーションとリサーチを綿密に行ってプロジェクトを理解しなければならない」と語る。プロジェクトの本質に迫る彼らの手法は、レコードレーベルの『Warp』や写真家のJuergen Teller、アーティストのMarc Quinn、ペンギンブックスなど、著名なクライアントたちを引きつけている。作品の骨太な印象とは裏腹に、サイモンの語り口は柔らか。「グラフィックデザインという言葉すら知らない頃から、コマーシャルアートが好きだった。いつもタイポグラフィーや写真、アートに興味があったから、この仕事をできていることがすごく嬉しいんだ」と謙虚な姿勢を見せる。スタジオ名からも伝わってくる、ポジティヴで前向きな姿勢も彼らの大きな魅力に違いない。

YES is known for their reductive and minimalist approach. Simon comments, "Our method is to pare down until the important message or elements are found. As a result of that you end up with a simple and elegant solution with a clear message. In order to do that, we must really understand the project through the process of research and collaboration." They obviously attract high-profile clients with this method of establishing the 'essence' of the project, building a client list including 'Warp' Records, Juergen Teller, artist Marc Quinn and Penguin Books. Simon speaks in a soft natured manner, a marked contrast to the some of the bolder work the studio produces. "I became interested in the area of 'commercial art' at a young age, possibly before I'd even heard the term 'graphic design'. I was always interested in typography, photography and art, so I feel very privileged to be doing what we do," revealing his modest outlook. This positive, straightforward attitude, something that is clearly reflected in their name, is surely a big part of their appeal.

A Foundation / Identity and Newsprint Publication

1

2

3

4

5

1. Moloko / Catalogue / Art Direction
2. Penguin Design Series / Book Covers
3. Gemma Booth / Website / gemmabooth.com
4. The Hi-Fi Series / Hand-Printed Serigraph
5. Dirty Vegas / Art Directon / Paintings by Richard Phillips

Warp20 / Art Direction / Photography by Dan Holdsworth

DESIGNERS MAP

過去・現在を俯瞰するUKデザイナーズ・マップ

1980年代以降に登場した著名なデザインスタジオを一挙に紹介。
代表的なスリーブデザインとともに、UKグラフィックデザインの過去30年を振り返る。

Peter Saville
www.petersaville.com

Malcolm Garrett
www.malcolmgarrett.com

NEVILLE BRODY
www.researchstudios.com

Vaughan Oliver
www.vaughanoliver.co.uk

Simon Halfon
www.simon-halfon.com

Me Company
www.mecompany.com

8vo

JONATHAN BARNBROOK
www.barnbrook.net

Ian Swift
www.swifty.co.uk

Blue Source

Nick Bell Design
www.nickbelldesign.co.uk

Phil Bains

INTRO
www.introwebsite.com

Trevor Jackson
www.trevor-jackson.com

Why Not Associates
www.whynotassociates.com

The Designers Republic
www.thedesignersrepublic.com

1990's

1980's

BIG ACTIVE
www.bigactive.com

Graphic Thought Facility
www.graphicthoughtfacility.com

Fuel Design
www.fuel-design.com

TOMATO
www.tomato.co.uk

Form
www.form.uk.com

Spin
www.spin.co.uk

STUDIO MYERSCOUGH
www.studiomyerscough.com

Slater Design
www.slaterdesign.co.uk

North
www.northdesign.co.uk

Farrow Design
www.farrowdesign.com

MIND DESIGN
www.minddesign.co.uk

Practise
www.practise.co.uk

NON-FORMAT
www.non-format.com

Andrew Townsend
www.andrew-townsend.com

Hypertype Studio
www.hypetype.co.uk

Airside
www.airside.co.uk

Sea Design
www.seadesign.co.uk

TOM HINGSTON STUDIO
www.hingston.net

Blast
www.blast.co.uk

Fluid
www.fluidesign.co.uk

Scott King
www.scottking.co.uk

Paul Barnes
www.moderntypography.com

Ben Drury

ÅBÄKE
www.kitsune.fr

MICHA WEIDMANN STUDIO
www.michaweidmannstudio.com

Tourist
www.wearetourist.com

MadeThought
www.madethought.com

Value and Service
www.valueandservice.co.uk

Hyperkit
www.hyperkit.co.uk

Build
www.designbybuild.com

Fraser Muggeridge studio
www.pleasedonotbend.co.uk

Saturday
www.saturday-london.com

BIBLIOTHÈQUE
www.bibliothequedesign.com

A Practice For Everyday Life
www.apracticeforeverydaylife.com

Sara De Bondt Studio
www.saradebondt.com

YES
www.yesstudio.co.uk

OWEN GILDERSLEEVE
www.owengildersleeve.com

JULIA
www.julia.uk.com

OK-RM
www.ok-rm.co.uk

Kate Moross
www.katemoross.com

WOOD McGRATH
www.woodmcgrath.com

IT'S NICE THAT
www.itsnicethat.com

EAT SLEEP WORK / PLAY
www.eatsleepworkplay.com

STUDIO 8
www.studio8design.co.uk

TAPPIN GOFTON
www.tappingofton.com

MELVIN GALAPON
www.mynameismelvin.co.uk

BRAVO CHARLIE MIKE HOTEL
www.bcmh.co.uk

Shaughnessy Works
www.shaughnessyworks.com

Universal Everything
www.universaleverything.com

2000'S

Q&A

22組のデザイナーに聞いた5つの質問

ÅBÄKE

1. –
2. Francis Upritchard
3. New Order "Power, Corruption and Lies"
4. –
5. –

BCMH (Bravo Charie Mike Hotel)

1. Fine Art, such as Bruno Munari and John Baldessari.
2. Bruno Munari, Niklaus Troxler
3. All Penguin Books Cover
4. Neutraface
5. RCA Secret

BIBLIOTHÈQUE

1. Stanley Kubrick, Diter Rams
2. Donald Judd
3. All Peter Saville's work
4. Univers
5. 72: Otl Aicher and the Munich Plumpiad, Adicolor Instalation

BIG ACTIVE

1. 60's New York Culture
2. Barney Bubble
3. Joy Division "Unknown Pleasures"
4. Baskerville
5. Beck "The Information" project

EAT SLEEP WORK / PLAY

1. –
2. –
3. XTC "Go 2"
4. Caslon
5. –

INTRO

1. Sonic Youth, Allen Ginsberg, Spacemen3
2. Peter Blake, Andy Warhol
3. Neu! "Neu!"
4. 60's Psychedelic Rock Hand-write Letter
5. Primal Scream "Xtrmntr" project

IT'S NICE THAT

1. Fine Art, David Carson
2. Paul Smith, John Baldessari
3. Pink Floyd "Dark Side of the Moon", Oasis "Definitely Maybe"
4. DIN (German Industrial Standard)
5. "If you could collaborate" show

JULIA

1. Valerio is more intro Brazilian Tropicana than Hugo, who is a fan of French Nouvelle Vague despite Erwan's taste for blockbusters.
2. Erwan: Cy Twombly and Saul Bass.
Hugo: Max Huber and Jean-Luc Godard.
Valerio: Sotsass and Pasolini.
3. –
4. –
5. Our final show at Royal College of Art

JONATHAN BARNBROOK

1. One is making the world a better place through design, both functionally and aesthetically. Another is letting people know the truth about the world. Also I do love typography, having a great way of showing the spirit of the time and being a place where there is still lots to experiment with.
2. I still think Picasso is the person who invented and added so much to contemporary visual art.
3. I really like Vaughan Oliver's work for Xmal Deutschland and Neville Brody's designs for Cabaret Voltaire.
4. Johnston, it's the one used on the London underground, it is based on classical proportions but is a modern serif.
5. The one I finished 10 years ago. I need some time to disconnect from the design process and understand whether work is good or not and it usually takes about 10 years to do that.

MELVIN GALAPON

1. Sci-Fi Movie "Tron"
2. Ian Wright.
3. Record Sleeve of "Simple Records"
4. Korinna
5. Show Off

MICHA WEIDMANN STUDIO

1. Anything but probably most of all is nature.
2. Rei Kawakubo, Richard Misarch, Wendelin Hess, James Turell, Piero Fornasetti…
3. The book cover "NINE SWIMMING POOLS" by Ed Ruscha
4. Poynter Display Demibold
5. An aerial photography project in California

1. What is your influence？ あなたに影響を与えているものを教えてください。

2. Who is your favorite designer / artist？ 好きなデザイナーまたはアーティストを教えてください。

3. Who is your favorite record sleeve / book cover？ 好きなレコードスリーブまたはブックカバーのデザインを教えてください。

4. What is your favorite font？ 好きなフォントを教えてください。

5. What is your favorite project？ これまでに手掛けた作品の中で、気に入っている作品を教えてください。

MIND DESIGN

1. Concrete Poetry
2. Josef Muller Brockmann
3. Sex Pistols "Never Mind The Bollocks"
4. –
5. Always latest one

OWEN GILDERSLEEVE

1. Music because I play the band.
2. Mario Hugo
3. Mike Perry's book cover work.
4. –
5. Recent few projects.

TOMATO

1. 7inch vinyl records at a moment
2. Nature
3. –
4. Serif and sans-serif
5. Maybe next one

NEVILLE BRODY

1. William S. Burroughs, Orson Welles, Throbbing Gristle, Cabaret Voltaire.
2. Aleksander Rodchenko, Max Huber, Peter Saville, Malcolm Garrett.
3. –
4. Helvetica
5. Always the project doing now.

STUDIO8

1. Every culture stuff.
2. –
3. All Pixies record cover and all Bluenote record cover.
4. –
5. –

TOM HINGSTON STUDIO

1. Martin Scorsese.
2. Robert Brownjohn, Hipnosis, Keiichi Tanaami.
3. Pink Floyd "Wish You Were Here" and The Beatles "The Beatles"
4. Coca-Cola Logo
5. Collaboration with Massive Attack

NON-FORMAT

1. Jon: Modernism of 50's, Sexiness of 60's, Post-Modernism of 70's, Earnestness of 80's, Irony of 90's, Infectious Neo-Folkness of 00's.
Kjell: Stanley Kubric "Epic 2001", David Bowie "Low", "Heroes" and "Diamond Dogs", Makoto Saito, Nick Knight, Andy Warhol.
2. Jon: Andy Warhol and Brian Eno
Kjell: Rem Koolhaas and Office for Metropolitan Architecture.
3. Jon: –
Kjell: Grace Jones "Living My Life"
4. Jon: Avant Garde
Kjell: Hermes
5. Jon: The Wire magazine
Kjell: Current project working on now.

STUDIO MYERSCOUGH

1. Billy Childish, Buff Medways and National Film Theatre.
2. Bridget Riley and tutor Geoff Fowle
3. –
4. Trade Gothic
5. the festival Future Vintage, Vintage at Goodwood

TAPPIN GOFTON

1. –
2. –
3. Peter Gabriel "1", "2", "3" and "4".
4. –
5. Coldplay "X&Y" project.

WOOD McGRATH

1. Suzy: I had an interest in all sorts of creative activities from an early age, but especially type and image.
2. Suzy&Martin: We don't have a favorite.
3. Suzy: An obscure English 7" sleeve issued in 1980, that features a simple black and white drawing by my father in law.
4. Suzy&Martin: That's an impossible question to answer. We discover new favourites regularly.
5. –

YES

1. Music: An Adrian Sherwood compilation by Paul from http://testpressing.org
Film: Cocksucker Blues by Robert Frank
Art: Richard Hamilton at the Serpentine Gallery
Book: New York Trilogy by Paul Auste
2. Andy Warhol
3. Joy Division "Unknown Pleasures"
4. Nobel
5. Always the current one

HELLO! UK GRAPHICS: Graphic Design in the UK since the 1980s
ハロー! UK グラフィックス：1980 年以降のグラフィックデザイン

2010 年 7 月 17 日　初版第 1 刷発行

著者	Rocket Company*/RCKT
編集	大山ゆかり（Rocket Company*/RCKT）
	工藤健士（Rocket Company*/RCKT）
	高宮 啓（Rocket Company*/RCKT）
	村上かおり（Rocket Company*/RCKT）
	高橋かおる（PIE BOOKS）
デザイン	藤本やすし（CAP）
	大嶽隆弘（CAP）
DTP	鈴木聖美
撮影	黒坂あけみ
撮影アシスタント	伊藤香織
翻訳	佐藤大輔
協力	パルコファクトリー
	D&AD
	ブリティッシュ・カウンシル
Author	Rocket Company*/RCKT
Edit	Yukari Ohyama (Rocket Company*/RCKT)
	Takeshi Kudo (Rocket Company*/RCKT)
	Akira Takamiya (Rocket Company*/RCKT)
	Kaori Murakami (Rocket Company*/RCKT)
	Kaoru Takahashi (PIE BOOKS)
Design	Yasushi Fujimoto (CAP)
	Takahiro Otake (CAP)
DTP	Kiyomi Suzuki
Photography	Akemi Kurosaka
Assistant	Kaori Kenny Ito
Translation	Daisuke Sato
Cooperation	PARCO FACTORY
	D&AD
	British Council
発行元	パイ インターナショナル
	〒 170-0005 東京都豊島区南大塚 2-32-4（東京支社）
	TEL: 03-3944-3981　FAX: 03-5395-4830
	sales@piebooks.com
	埼玉県蕨市北町 1-19-21-301（本社）
制作協力	PIE BOOKS
印刷・製本	Daiichi Publishers Co. Ltd
Publisher	PIE International Inc.
	2-32-4 Minami-Otsuka, Toshima-ku, Tokyo 170-0005 JAPAN
	sales@pie-intl.com
Publishing support	PIE BOOKS
Printing	Daiichi Publishers Co. Ltd